THE
ART
OF
INDOOR
BONSAI

THE ART OF INDOOR BONSAI

Cultivating Tropical, Sub-tropical and Tender Bonsai

John Ainsworth
Photographs by Bob Challinor

Trafalgar Square Publishing
NORTH POMFRET, VERMONT

First published in the United States of America
in 1989 by Trafalgar Square Publishing,
North Pomfret, Vermont 05053

First paperback edition 1992
Reprinted 1993, 1994
First published in Great Britain in 1988
by Ward Lock, London

Text © John Ainsworth 1988, 1992
Photographs © Ward Lock 1988, 1992
Line drawings © Ward Lock 1988, 1992

House editor Denis Ingram
Designed by David Allen
Text filmset/set in Palatino/Gill Sans
by Tradespools Ltd, Frome, Somerset

Library of Congress Catalog Card Number 92-80484

ISBN 0 943955 58 0

Printed and bound in Hong Kong
by Wing King Tong Co Ltd

Dedication and author's acknowledgements

This book is dedicated to my wife Jean who
persuaded me to write it. Also to my mother
Ros and to Nichola and Peter.

My sincere and especial thanks to the lady I put
under considerable pressure to type the ms –
Theresa.

Thanks are also due to the staff of Tokonoma
Bonsai Ltd., particularly 'Ed' who put up with
my moods during the writing, and to Gerrit
and Hanako Lodder and to Frank Zwart, who
helped with four of the photographs.

Frontispiece *Chinese-style landscape on
rock planted with a five-year-old* Ehretia
(Carmona).

Contents

Preface
page 6

PART 1
Cultivation,
Care and Training

1. Introduction and history
page 8

2. Care of indoor bonsai trees
page 12

3. Styles of bonsai
page 24

4. Propagation
page 30

5. Training indoor bonsai
page 36

6. Repotting indoor bonsai
page 46

7. Special effects
page 52

8. Pests and diseases
page 54

PART 2
A–Z
Selection of Tropical,
Sub-tropical and Tender Bonsai
page 58

Index
page 127

Preface

This is a book about indoor bonsai trees grown in temperate, sub-tropical or tropical regions.

Bonsai trees are grown in pots, which are normally fairly shallow, and not in the open ground. By changing their habitat from ground to pot, the effect upon them of temperature change, sunshine etc., is greatly altered. Trees and shrubs that are normally thought of as hardy (resistant to frost damage) are not necessarily so when they are grown in a false environment. You will find I have described certain varieties of trees and shrubs that are normally thought of as hardy as being tender temperate or even sub-tropical. For example, some elms and zelkovas come from sub-tropical regions such as South China and Taiwan; they have adapted to grow in colder climates but it is not their original environment. The phrases tender temperate, sub-tropical and tropical are, however, not just an indication of the tree's origin. They should also be a guide as to what temperature and conditions the tree prefers.

Chinese *Zelkova*, *Buxus*, *Pyracantha*, *Nandina*, *Podocarpus* and *Styrax* are usually considered hardy, but grown as bonsai in a pot they need to be protected from the frost and are thus described as tender temperate or sub-tropical. As a director of Tokonoma Bonsai Ltd., I can assure the reader that I remember with pain what happened to these so-called 'hardy' trees in the winters of 1985/6 and 1986/7. It is through bitter experience we now know which trees should be regarded as tender temperate.

As a grower of indoor bonsai please trust my recommendations as far as temperatures etc., are concerned. They have been tried and found to be successful.

J. A.

PART I

Cultivation,
Care and Training

An air-layered plant showing plentiful root growth.

CHAPTER 1

Introduction and history

This book is written to tell you all about the growing of indoor bonsai, wherever you happen to live. Hopefully it will not only instruct and teach, but it will also inspire you to try this fascinating hobby for yourself.

As most people realize, the translation of the word 'bonsai' is simply a plant grown in a container. It does not define what type of plant or what sort of container. It also does not tell the novice bonsai grower of the many hours of happiness to be obtained by lovingly caring for and training your own bonsai trees. This you will find out for yourself.

Although most of us naturally associate the growing of bonsai with the Chinese and Japanese, envisaging a perfectly trained miniature tree, it is as well to go back to the actual origins of bonsai training so that we can understand some of the philosophy that their care and cultivation must incorporate.

Returning to the original definition of bonsai, let us consider plants in containers. Compared with earlier civilizations, it is only fairly recently that people in the West have appreciated having plants in their homes. Although the beginning of pot plant cultivation as such is virtually lost in the mists of time, most historians believe that it was the Chinese who originally started growing plants in pots, for the Emperor's gardens. The Chinese have always been a mystical people and it is believed that they considered a lot of plants they grew had almost magical qualities, and indeed that some of them were inhabited by spirits or gods. Their fascination with nature is seen in ancient Chinese prints and in their poetry and other writings, where plants as well as wind carved rocks often feature.

The next direct evidence of plants being grown in man-made containers comes from Egypt between three and four thousand years ago. Here holes were carved in rock and trees planted in them. At this particular time in history gardens were becoming increasingly popular and it was not uncommon for certain plants to be transplanted from one place to another. Gardeners of the day soon discovered that by enclosing the root ball in a rudimentary pot, they could transplant trees and plants with the least possible disturbance to their growth.

Among the so-called 'Seven Wonders' of the ancient world were the Hanging Gardens of Babylon, which featured many plants that had been transported from other locations. Many of them were also growing in containers fashioned by man.

Another example comes from India where healers and magicians used to grow young specimens of various types of jungle tree such as the *Ficus* (fig) and *Tamarindus* (tamarind) for medicinal purposes. If they were not living near to where these natural medicines grow normally, they found it necessary to transplant into containers younger and smaller trees so that they could have them close at hand. These were also among the first known potted plants.

Beginnings of bonsai

How did it start?
There is a long history of dispute over whether the Chinese or Japanese were the originators of bonsai and which of them first started training bonsai trees. However, what is meant by training? Is it the bonsai tree that we see today – the one that has been perfected by many years of careful root, leaf and branch pruning? It could be suggested the actual origins of bonsai, as we know them today, occurred almost by accident.

If you have a plant in your house that is growing strongly and becomes too large for its position, you have a number of options. The first is to move it somewhere else. The second is to give it to a relative or friend who has a large house and likes plants. On the other hand, you could throw it away; but but you are not going to do that because you are fond of it – perhaps a favourite relative gave it to you years ago, or it reminds you of some special occasion. However, if none of these alternatives is available to you, one way of being able to keep this plant is to prune it.

Pruning in this particular instance simply means reducing the whole of the plant to a more manageable size; out come a pair of secateurs and you quickly remove unwanted growth. The whole family is pleased because they can now move around the sitting-room, see the television and feel the sunlight coming in without this enormous plant getting in the way! However, then comes another consideration. If you had pruned it slightly differently would it have looked better? Without realizing it, your thoughts are turning to the art of bonsai, even though you might know little or nothing about their training.

We would find the origins of bonsai by taking your present day thoughts and transposing them to a small household somewhere in China, India or Japan, thousands of years ago. You should begin to see that the Japanese meaning for bonsai as 'a plant in a container' has been slightly altered.

It is almost certain that people both in the East and West now regard a more fitting translation of bonsai, as being a *miniaturized* plant, shrub, or tree in a container – the process of miniaturization being achieved by planting in a smaller than normal container and by judicious pruning.

Indoor bonsai

The term 'indoor bonsai' could be used to define a bonsai tree not growing in its normal habitat. To understand why this is so, consider the steps needed to be taken to protect less hardy trees by people living in temperate climates. In this sort of climate the four seasons are distinct: the summers are hopefully warm, and the winter temperature often falls below freezing. A tree that originates from tropical or sub-tropical regions cannot survive under frosty conditions. It must, therefore, be given protection during the cold months. Although some people are fortunate enough to have greenhouses that are heated, for the majority of us there is only one option if we are to successfully look after bonsai trees, which are trained in hotter climates: by necessity we have to bring them into our houses during the winter months.

On the other hand many people live in regions in the world where the temperature never falls below freezing. For them, snow and ice is something only to be read about and seen in pictures. But what about excessive heat? In these same regions the outside temperature may be so hot at times that for comfort people will need to install air conditioning. This brings us to wider definition of indoor trees and one that is not normally considered in temperate regions. If a tree is used to a temperate climate, with four distinct seasons, it will have trouble thriving in a hot climate. In such cases it is again necessary to try and duplicate the tree's normal growing conditions, i.e. make the conditions considerably colder in winter than in summer. It is possible to keep temperate trees in the hotter climates as long as these conditions can be met.

The first thing to realize is that the temperature difference between summer and winter in temperate climates is considerable. Secondly, and of equal importance but quite often forgotten, is that day length during summer and winter in temperate areas also varies. This is not such a vital factor in tropical regions. Some degree of artificial lighting is often necessary for tropical trees when they are moved to a colder climate and, to a lesser extent, for temperate trees in more tropical regions where, during the trees' normal summer, their day length is much longer than that experienced by trees from more equatorial regions.

The care of indoor bonsai in our homes will be looked at in greater detail later in the book.

Criticisms against bonsai

Criticism has sometimes been levelled at the bonsai grower that bonsai trees are not natural; that their forms are often grotesque and the very growing of these miniaturized trees is, in fact, cruel.

Bonsai as unnatural
In the majority of cases bonsai trees and shrubs are miniaturized versions of those growing in gardens and in the wild. They are not genetic dwarfs. In many instances small herbs, grasses, etc., are also planted to complement the form of the tree. Miniature conifers and shrubs are, generally speaking, used only to produce Mame (among the smallest bonsai, and less than 15 cm or 6 in in height) and to plant miniature landscapes, called 'Saikei' in Japan.

As a bonsai grower, you have taken a normally large or medium-size growing tree and adapted it to grow in a relatively small pot. As such, it has to be admitted that at first glance the growing of bonsai trees does not appear natural to the species being used. However, if one looks around at our modern day world how much of what we see and do is entirely natural? If you were to carry this desire for naturalness to its extreme then you would not live in a house, your hair would be long and matted, men's beards would be long and unshaven, and women would not wear make-up.

As far as plant material is concerned, very little grown today could be called 'natural' in the true sense of the word: most plants are now hybridized to produce either a greater yield of grain, or to give different colour flowers or leaves, etc. Likewise, a lot of fruit trees and other ornamental flowering trees are propagated by grafting. This is to ensure a healthy strong root on an otherwise desirable plant that quite often is weaker if grown on its natural roots.

Grotesque shapes
The criticism that bonsai are not natural and are, in fact, grotesque, can be linked. At the end of the 19th century and at the beginning of the 20th century,

when bonsai became of more general interest to people in the West, it was the practice to grow many trees in what we would now consider to be ugly and unnatural styles. One of the favourite ways of training trees in China in those days was to grow them in the form of 'lucky' characters from the Chinese language. In Japan the training could involve gross twisting in the style of a sort of octopus, and to be formalized to such an extent that they eventually bore no resemblance to their larger counterparts and were mere caricatures in appearance. This practice has now virtually ceased, although in some areas of China trees are still grown to look relatively unusual. (This normally occurs in the northern regions of China where the extraordinary trunks of some trees are highly prized.)

Around the world today, bonsai growers more often than not train trees to look as natural as possible. Indeed, their training becomes a glorification of nature and not a travesty. This does not, however, preclude growers from producing trees in, say, the cascade style that at first glance look somewhat out of place. These are all trained, however, to reflect the growing of trees in nature.

A few years ago one would attend exhibitions and hear a comment like 'Oh dear, they look like little Chinese ladies with their feet bound'. Then would inevitably follow the remark, 'I think they are fascinating, but I don't like them because it is cruel'. This actually shows a complete lack of understanding of how bonsai trees are grown and trained. To the bonsai grower, far from the tree appearing unnatural, each different type of tree evokes the beauty and cruelty of nature in the raw. A *Ficus* (java willow, weeping fig) that has been trained to grow over a stone or rock can take one back hundreds of years to the depths of the jungle in Cambodia to see its wilder cousins with roots completely entwining the ancient temples of Ankar Wat, and now growing to the roof of the jungle. Bonsai trees cultivated in the Middle East or Mediterranean regions can often remind one of many happy days spent on holiday. By looking around a little, wild versions of *Pistacia* (pistachio) and *Pinus halepensis* (Aleppo pine) can be seen in their natural habitat.

Have a close look at these trees; even sketch or photograph them. These become invaluable to the bonsai enthusiast, showing him how the indoor trees he has at home grow in the wild. Obviously one does not have to copy their form exactly, but it is always a useful starting point to growing natural-looking trees. Also note the habitat in which they are growing. *Pistacia* (pistachio), *Olea* (olive) and *Pinus halepensis* (Aleppo pine) will often be seen growing near the sea. This will indicate that these varieties are resistant to sea air, and can therefore be grown successfully in temperate areas close to sea water.

Although when looking at an ancient olive or fig tree one cannot help but admire their twisted trunks and, in the case of figs, their aerial roots; it is none the less true that the larger the tree the more difficult it is to appreciate one small leaf or one small flower. This is one of the joys of bonsai. One can admire a single twig or leaf as easily as the whole magnificent tree.

In the Far East bonsai was, and to a certain extent still is, related to the philosophy and religion of both Taoism and Buddhism. The attempt is made to create a symmetry between man and nature. In some instances bonsai become a stylized fragment of nature that only the bonsai artist (for such he is) can see and appreciate. However, you do not need to be a master of bonsai to gain pleasure from watching their growth and development. Don't forget that every tree is different; you will never find two identical trees, whether as bonsai or growing in the wild.

The art of bonsai growing

In some countries the training of bonsai is regarded as an art form, and this simile between art and bonsai can be enlarged upon. If you consider that training a tree is similar to putting paint onto canvas, and that the pot represents the frame, you will see what is meant by bonsai being an art form.

If all trees grew in exactly the same way then bonsai could be taught in the same way as painting and one could perhaps do a copy of a 'masterpiece' by numbers. Although these pictures might give a pleasing effect they are similar, in a way, to potted flowering plants that are extremely difficult to tell apart. With bonsai, the person who is training and cultivating their own trees is able to use all of his or her imagination to produce a beautiful tree.

Cost

Another criticism of bonsai is their expensive price. Why is this? To revert back to our simile with painting, we might also ask why a collection of paints applied to a canvas sometimes fetches hundreds of thousands – if not millions – of pounds, whereas the initial costs of these materials are minute in comparison. The reason is that the paint has been applied in such a manner as to make the paintings masterpieces of the art world. In contrast your picture that has been painted by numbers is worth, to be frank, little more than the cost of the materials. In the case of both the picture and the bonsai tree one is paying for the imagination and skill of the artist.

It should also be borne in mind that bonsai can take many, many years to perfect. One can, on the other hand, achieve very pleasing results with young stock grown in a pot for little more than a year. The price applied to smaller non-mature trees, is also tiny in comparison to that asked for very ancient, very beautiful, trees. To what does one aspire? To a Constable or Rembrandt perhaps? So be it if you have the necessary money; you will certainly derive a great deal of satisfaction from your purchase. However if, like most of us, these masterpieces are not within your price range, you may well be just as happy with something that is less valuable on paper.

Bonsai versus topiary

An interesting comparison has been made between the Western idea of topiary and that of training bonsai. Topiary takes the form of clipped yew trees, or other similar evergreen trees, fashioned into all manner of different shapes, such as peacocks, chess pieces, elephants, people, etc. In a sense, one is sculpting alternative forms from living plant material. Bonsai, on the other hand, attempts to recreate a diminutive version of a real tree, and not to produce some shape that is entirely alien to that tree.

The appeal of bonsai

The fascination with the miniature goes back many hundreds, if not thousands of years in the Far East, and over a number of decades it has become of increasing interest and popularity in the Western world. There can be many reasons for this interest but probably not least is the fact that with the increasing number of people living in smaller houses and flats, often in congested towns, there are fewer opportunities to appreciate nature in the raw. This in mind, what could be more appealing than miniature trees that stand in their own little world upon a table near a window, evoking memories of distant places and warmer climates?

One particular misunderstanding about bonsai has to be countered. When bonsai from the Far East were originally exhibited in London in 1909 people were fascinated by their forms. Unfortunately all of these trees subsequently died. From that and from other unlucky experiences has come the idea that there is an ancient mystical Eastern secret to growing them successfully. This simply is not true, and I shall attempt to show you how these trees can be kept easily and happily in the home.

Bonsai require much less attention than people usually think. Their care requires a few minutes a day, just the same as ordinary house plants, to check whether they need watering, etc. Provided this is done and they are positioned correctly, they can take as little or as much of any other spare time you have.

Sageretia, *approximately 45 years old, 40 cm (16 in) tall. Secondary planting of* Sasa *(dwarf bamboo).*

CHAPTER 2

Care of indoor bonsai trees

Approximate disposition of trees around the world

Equatorial and tropical trees can be found in latitudes roughly 35° south across the equator to 35° north.

Sub-tropical trees grow from 25°–45° of latitude both north and south. The regions included here are South Australia, Africa and America, as well as the Mediterranean, Southern United States, the Middle East, China, etc.

Temperate trees grow from 35°–55° of latitude north and south. This includes southernmost Australia, South Africa, as well as mid Europe, Japan and much of the United States of America and Canada (Fig. 1).

It must be remembered that this is a very rough guide. Temperatures can differ greatly depending on whether you live by the sea or further inland. The further away from the sea, in large land masses such as China and the United States of America, the greater will be the changes in temperature

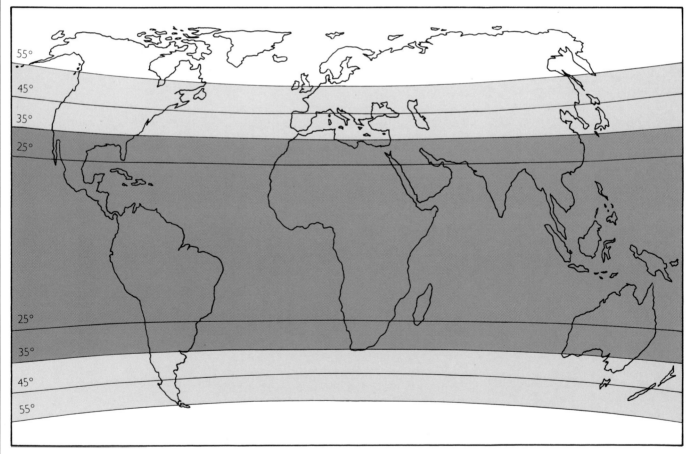

Fig. 1 *Outline map of world showing latitudes which embrace temperate, sub-tropical and tropical regions.*

throughout the year. Other factors such as prevailing winds, currents, whether the situation is in a valley or on top of a mountain, should also be taken into account.

By careful observation you should soon realize the type of trees that occur in your locality and which should be kept indoors.

Tropical trees

These include *Ficus* vars., *Cycas*, *Sageretia*, *Carmona*, *Zelkova* (Chinese), *Murraya*, *Rhapis,Jacaranda*, *Tamarind*, *Schefflera*, *Sterculia* and many others – in fact all trees and shrubs that originate from tropical regions.

Favourable temperatures

When considering the temperature and other requirements of trees, it is as well to remember the area in the world from which they originate. Tropical trees and shrubs are used to high temperatures that remain fairly constant throughout the year. They do, however, decrease by a few degrees during the night. The optimum temperature for tropical trees is between 15° C (60° F) and 27° C (80° F). If these trees are kept near an exterior window, but not between a heavy curtain and single glazing as this area will become too cold during the night, then their temperature will naturally reduce during the darker hours by the required amount. Tropical trees will survive at lower temperatures, but these should not be maintained for extended periods. As a general rule, between 10 and 15° C (50–50° F) is the absolute safe minimum to maintain healthy growth.

Please remember that if your house is situated in a cold region and the central heating is on a time switch, so that it turns off during the day or night when it is not required, then it is essential to maintain the minimum temperatures mentioned above. Under no circumstances should tropical trees ever be subjected to temperatures below freezing. They will invariably suffer and some varieties will die almost immediately. During the summer months, when day length in temperate regions is extended and temperatures are maintained above the suggested minimum of 10° C (50° F), then tropical trees can safely be put outside for rest and recuperation.

As previously mentioned few, if any, of the trees and shrubs grown as indoor bonsai have originated in the atmosphere of a modern day home. A brief period outside in the fresh air, protected from excessive wind and shaded from excess sunshine, will cheer them up immensely. It might sound a contradiction in terms to suggest that long hours of sunlight could damage tropical trees, but please don't forget that some, though not all, of these varieties grow in the shade provided by their larger cousins. Their day length, however intense the sunlight, is only about twelve hours. It should also be remembered that these trees are growing in relatively small pots; as such they can dry out extremely quickly. Providing a certain amount of shade, especially during the hot afternoon sunlight, does them no harm at all and will help you to maintain healthy trees.

Light levels and day length

Tropical trees are, on the whole, used to much higher light levels than trees growing in temperate or even sub-tropical regions. Do not confuse light levels with the strength of direct sunlight. Very few plants except for, say, cactus and *Sterculia rupestris* (bottle tree) are happy directly beside the glass of a south-facing window. Even in winter the light intensity can be strong, and the temperature greatly increased with the magnifying effect of the sun passing through the glass. The ideal position for tropical trees within the home, is up to 1.5 m (5 ft) away from a window that receives partial sunlight up to approximately four hours a day. However, they can stand directly on a windowsill near to a radiator if the window is not situated where it receives direct sunlight for more than about half an hour a day.

If neither of these positions are possible, and your trees have to be in an area of lower light intensity, it might be worth investing in a light metre. You will be amazed how quickly light levels (lux) decrease the further away from a window one goes (Fig. 2). It is difficult for the human eye to measure this, but tropical trees are super sensitive to such a variation. If it is found that the light level is lower than approximately 700 lux – this is normally in a position of about 2.4–3 m (8–10 ft) away from a fairly large bright window – then it may become necessary to supplement natural light with lamps that are designed especially for this purpose. Many garden centres and electrical shops now supply these 'Gro Lights'. They are comparatively cheap and easy to install, and a time switch can be incorporated into the circuit to provide a constant day length throughout the year, day in day out, which tropical trees are used to. Please note that it is only away from the equator that we have differing day and night lengths, depending on the time of the year. On the equator the day length is 12 hours, and the night length is 12 hours, 365 days of the year.

Tropical flowering trees will benefit from periods of sunshine when they are coming into flower. As a rough guide remember that variegated trees, and trees with small leaves, require bright conditions but with little or no sunlight. Pure foliage trees with larger green leaves need slightly less bright conditions, and over a period of time they can adapt to positions of semi-shade.

Position

The position in the home where you keep your tropical bonsai trees will depend on where you can maintain the temperatures and light levels as mentioned previously. To get the best from your trees, not only for their health, but also for your own pleasure and enjoyment, it helps to have a permanent display where you can enjoy them at any time. Here they become a feature on their own, and will be a constant source of interest.

Another advantage of having your own collection of tropical bonsai is that you can still appreciate the greenery and growth of living trees during the winter months when the countryside outside your home is bare and dismal. Provided the conditions for temperature and light have been met, then the only other thing to guard against are draughts.

A draught is air moving rapidly from one area to another. Most obviously this can be caused by open doors or windows, but quite severe cold draughts can also occur around the edges and underneath doors and ill-fitting windows. Nearly all trees, and especially tropical trees, will suffer in temperate homes where draughts occur.

If your centrally-heated home has a particularly dry

Fig. 2 Diagram showing positions for trees in a typical room.
A = This area is too dark for most trees. Supplementary lighting will be needed.
B = Trees that do not mind subdued light can be displayed on this table.
C = Ideal for sub-tropical trees here.
D = Ideal for tropical trees here. At least 30 cm (1 ft) above radiator.

atmosphere, you can invest in an electrical humidifier to keep the humidity at a constant level.

It is also a good idea to construct an attractive stand outside, on which to display your bonsai trees in summer. If you are lucky you will be able to position this so that you can see your trees from some of the windows of your home.

A lot of people that have tropical trees also have trees from more temperate regions, and will probably already have a suitable stand. This can be constructed of almost any materials that are available but it should be partially shaded, not by large trees, but by lathes or some other suitable wood or plastic net that will give the trees up to about 50% shade (Fig. 3). This is done for a number of reasons: it cuts down the excessive drying effect of afternoon sunshine, as well

A group of miniature indoor bonsai.

Fig. 3 *Outside display.*

as helping to deflect high winds and heavy rain. Shading, in fact, makes life for the bonsai grower just that little bit easier.

During the summer months it is advisable to give most of your tropical trees a treat and allow them to stay outside on their stand for as long as possible. This does not, of course, stop you displaying trees indoors, as they can take turns in being admired inside the home. This is also the time of the year when outdoor trees can safely be brought in for brief periods, provided they are given sufficient light.

Watering

How do you know how often to water a tropical tree? In my experience watering has become almost as much of a mystery to the new bonsai enthusiast as it is to know when and how to prune roots. In Japan and China bonsai masters still say it can take up to three years to learn how to water a tree properly. However, their instruction often takes the form of asking the student to just look and learn. They do not necessarily tell people the few basic and simple rules that I hope will help you overcome this problem.

No plants – not even desert cacti or air plants – survive in nature without absorbing a certain amount of moisture, although the method of absorption may differ. Many tropical trees, in fact, require a high humidity level and frequent watering, especially

during the growing season. The method of providing the humidity that these plants require to survive in the modern day centrally-heated home is fairly simple, but it must be adhered to. It is suggested that you stand your tropical bonsai on a piece of wood (Fig. 4) surrounded by wet gravel within a plastic or ceramic tray. You can, of course, stand the tree directly on the gravel, but if it is left in this position for an extended period the roots will grow through the drainage holes in the pot and into the gravel. In this case they would have to be removed at regular intervals. To encourage them to remain within the pot, stand your trees on rocks or pieces of wood, which themselves stand on the gravel.

Tropical trees should never be allowed to dry out. Two methods of watering are normally used for house plants: the first, and probably the most common, is to use a small watering can (Fig. 5). However, as composts used for bonsai trees differ to those used for ordinary house plants, there is another more satisfactory method. Normal tap water that has been allowed to stand overnight in a bowl, thus expelling harmful chemicals as well as adjusting to room temperature, is perfectly adequate in most instances. If one has the facilities for collecting rainwater, this is even more beneficial provided, once again, it has been allowed to adjust its temperature to that of the room in which the trees are growing. Your tropical bonsai can then be immersed in this water up to or even over the rim of the pot for approximately

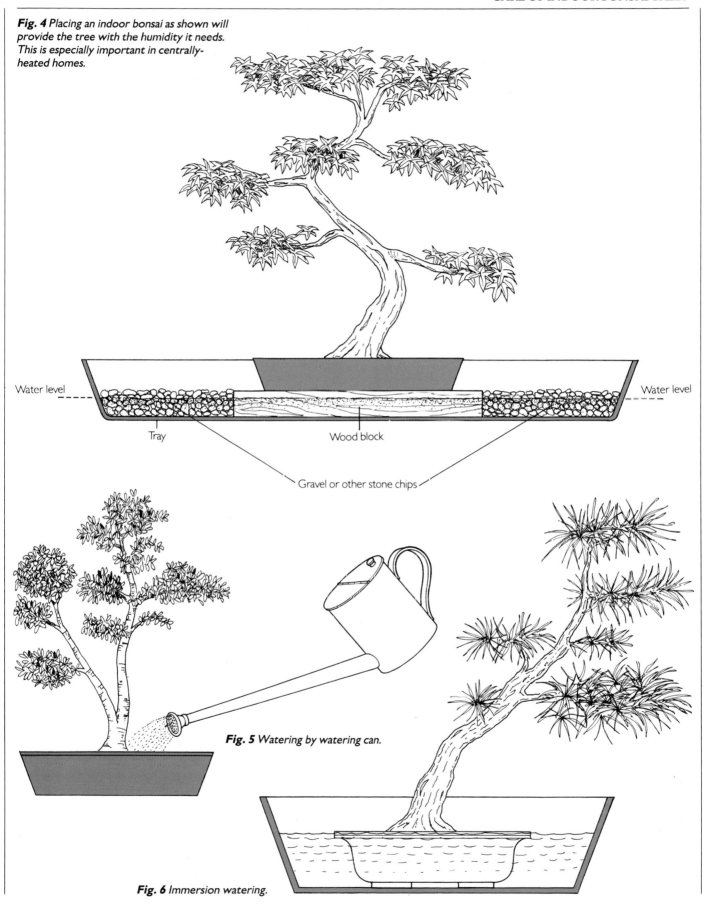

Fig. 4 *Placing an indoor bonsai as shown will provide the tree with the humidity it needs. This is especially important in centrally-heated homes.*

Water level

Water level

Tray

Wood block

Gravel or other stone chips

Fig. 5 *Watering by watering can.*

Fig. 6 *Immersion watering.*

20 minutes whenever watering is needed (Fig.6).

The benefits of watering by immersion are quite considerable. The main disadvantage to watering with a watering can is that if the plant has become drier than it should be, then the compost has the tendency to shrink. When this occurs a gap is formed between the compost and the pot itself. The water that you pour over the top of the root ball will tend to dissipate down around the sides of the pot and go straight out of the drainage holes at the bottom. Sometimes it appears that the tree has been well watered because the top of the soil is damp; however the inside of the root ball can remain as dry as it was before. By immersing the whole pot, the water is taken up through the drainage holes and, after being left for a shortish length of time, the initially dry root ball will absorb the moisture that it needs and expand again to meet the sides of the pot.

When watering, it is also important not to give water in drips and drabs. Give the tree ample water whenever it is needed. After it has been watered, it should be removed and the excess water be allowed to drain off before being returned to its display position.

To add a further complication to the mystery of watering, trees can be damaged by excessive watering. This is especially so during the winter months of a temperate climate when, despite artificial warmth and light, the tree will slow down its growth and become semi dormant. The golden rule is if your tree has compost that looks pale or feels dry or even dusty to the touch, then it is time to water. If the compost is still moist, and you have been watering by the immersion method, then the tree should not be watered further.

You will find that all trees, including tropical trees, will not need as much water during the winter months as they do during the summer, unless the atmosphere in which they are being kept is excessively hot.

Symptoms of underwatering, and too little humidity
The first symptom of underwatering with broad leaf trees is that the leaves will flag or droop. Flowers can often then fall quicker than normal. Leaf tips and edges become yellow, and eventually brown. In extreme cases they will become completely brown and fall. On other trees the leaves might not go crisp and brown before falling. In this instance the older leaves, followed shortly by the younger leaves, will fall off altogether but without changing colour at all.

To be able to tell whether needle trees are getting the water that they need, is next to impossible. Occasionally the needle tips will turn brown. If this is seen, then watering should be stepped up immediately.

Symptoms of too much water, and too high humidity
One of the symptoms of too much water in a root ball

or in the surrounding air is that, again, leaves become limp and lifeless looking. However they do not normally become crisp. One of the best ways of checking whether or not a tree is being given too much moisture is by lifting the whole thing out of its container. Look at the roots. Scratch the surface of one or pull off one of the smaller roots. If they appear rotten then the possibility is that it is being given too much water. In a normal healthy tree you should see white root tips growing nearly the whole year round except for in the darkest, coldest part of the winter, when even tropical trees are resting to a certain extent.

Another bad sign is to see grey mould appearing on the trees, especially if this mould or rot occurs around the leaf axils and on young shoots.

Feeding

In the past some people considered the way to train bonsai trees was to underwater them and to starve them of all nutrients in order to keep them small. This is a complete fallacy. Bonsai trees are miniaturized versions of larger trees. When one pots up a bonsai, whether it is in a conventional pot, planted over a stone, or even planted on a single slab of rock, we have to produce as nearly as possible its native growing conditions. All trees require air circulation around the roots as well as water. This air circulation is essential for healthy growth. They also require nutrients to keep them healthy, just as they would in the wild. The nutrients a tree needs occur in most present day composts, but only to a certain degree. They will, after a period of time, leach out of the compost because of the action of watering and the fact that the tree will be taking them up when they are needed for its growth.

The three most essential ingredients in any fertilizer are as follows:
Nitrogen (N) This is the most well known constituent of all fertilizers. Nitrogen is responsible for growth above the ground. If applied in correct quantities, it keeps the leaves green, and the tree growing properly.
Phosphates (P_2O_5) Phosphates produce healthy, vigorous roots on the trees, enabling those roots to transfer water and other nutrients to the upper part of the tree.
Potash (K_2O) Potash, amongst other things, produces healthy flowers, giving them good colour, etc.

If one examines chemical fertilizers in a garden centre or shop, you will see by looking at the varied percentages of each of the above three essential elements that they are formulated for different purposes. A high nitrogen fertilizer is designed to make the plant grow strongly, a low nitrogen, high potash and phosphate fertilizer is used to encourage

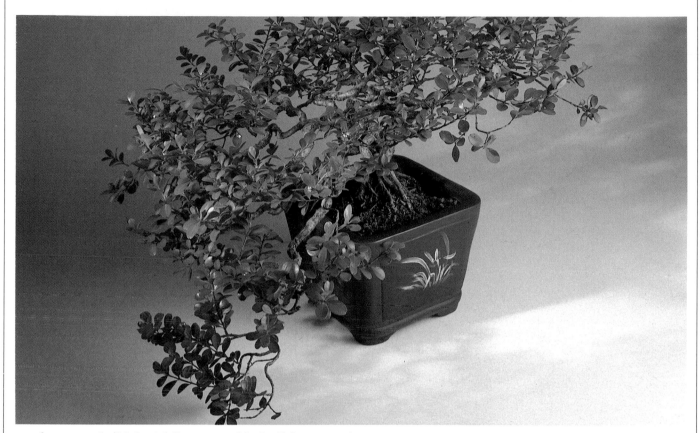

Buxus, *showing coiled style from China, 50 cm (20 in) tall.*

good roots and a high yielding crop of fruit. Other trace elements normally found in good quality fertilizers are magnesium oxide, iron, manganese, zinc, boron, and molybdenum.

How you feed your trees is entirely up to you. Some people believe in pure organic fertilizer. This has the effect of being slower to release in the compost, but has the advantage of being purely organic. On the other hand, inorganic fertilizers have advanced so much in composition, as well as release time, in the last few years, that these can be equally as effective. Granulated fertilizer that releases over a period of six to 12 months is now in use throughout the horticultural industry. This can be mixed with your own initial compost, and only needs renewing once a year. However the disadvantage of this is that it is released constantly over this period. Perhaps the best form of inorganic fertilizer is one that can be applied as a liquid, not only to feed the root system, but also to feed the leaves directly.

As a general rule fertilizer is given throughout the growing season, but not when trees are inactive. As tropical trees have very short dormant seasons, fertilizer can be applied to them almost throughout the year, although this should be considerably reduced during the winter months. Trees that flower should also not have fertilizer for a month before they come into flower, until the flowers drop, and until the fruits, if any, are well formed.

For many years the Japanese have used organic fertilizers in pelleted form that are pushed into the top of the compost and left there throughout the season. This gives a slow release of fertilizer, but the disadvantage for indoor trees is that it can form mould and sometimes gives off an unpleasant 'natural' smell.

If one reads the older books on growing bonsai trees successfully, you might be forgiven for being thoroughly confused by some of the constituents with which it is suggested you feed your trees. A tree takes up the nutrients that are available in whatever form they are. Although trees are beautiful and fascinating living things, they are not able to tell the difference between where these nutrients come from: soya beans, fishmeal, wood ash, and cotton seed, are not essential to their growth. For ease of application, unless the grower knows a lot about organic fertilizers, it is suggested that powdered or granulated inorganic fertilizer is ideal for nearly all applications. This also removes the rather inexact science of mixing your own organic fertilizer and, by careful selection, the formula you need can easily be found.

Not enough fertilizer
The best tell-tale signs of this are that leaves appear paler than they should and take on a listless appearance. Growth is slow, and insects attack readily. Flowering trees will also have fewer flowers than normal.

Too much fertilizer

Fertilizer that has been applied too strongly can cause a similar apperance to not enough water in as much that leaf edges can become brown and crisp, looking scorched. Spots can also appear on the leaves. Overall growth of the tree, especially during heavy periods of rain, can be excessive. Leaves may also become much larger than normal.

Holiday care

During periods when one is absent from the home during the winter months, the heating will have to be kept on in the room in which your tropical bonsai are displayed, but this can be lowered to the minimum requirements. Lowering the temperature will also cut down the need for watering, although some provision must be made to give the tree sufficient water during the period that you are absent.

One way of conserving water for some smaller trees is to put the whole thing, tree and pot, into a plastic bag (Fig.7). If you blow the bag up and tie the top so that no air escapes, you will not need to support the bag. However, you should try to stop it touching the leaves as this might cause mildew. I have tried this method myself and I have found a tree can last a number of weeks in its own plastic greenhouse.

If you are only going to be absent for a few days, say up to a week, then a tray full of water in which to sit the tree can be used. Provided the temperature has been lowered as suggested, it will not need further watering whilst you are away. If you are to be away for longer periods then other ways can be used. Reservoirs of water with very thin pipes (Fig.8) coming from them which can be adjusted so that they drip at regular intervals onto the compost, are obtainable from garden centres, and although they are quite expensive they are very effective. Another

Fig. 7 *Moisture retention with plastic bag.*

Fig. 9 *Two methods of watering with wicks.*

Fig. 8 *'Shoelace' watering from reservoir.*

method is to have a bowl of water next to your tree with a homemade wick going from the water into the compost of the tree (Fig.9). This is comparatively cheap, but it is not as effective as a reservoir.

If you have reliable relatives or neighbours you may like to entrust the job of watering your precious bonsai trees to them. However, make sure they are aware how often the trees need to be watered. If you are fortunate enough to be near a specialist bonsai nursery, then they will be only too happy to care for your trees in your absence. They normally charge very little for this service, and you will be able to go away knowing that your trees are in expert hands.

During the summer when you are away on holiday, correct watering is even more critical. Naturally enough the temperature in the summer is higher than that in the winter. Humidity levels in the summer are also considerably lower. This means that your tree, which is in active growth, will need watering far more frequently. Trees in very shallow or comparatively small containers can quite often need watering once or twice a day wherever they are being kept. During the summer, if your trees are outside they should be shaded and protected from as much strong wind as possible. Remember, too, that during this time they will dry out quicker outside than they will in a cool room, such as the bathroom of your house.

Sub-tropical trees

These include *Citrus* vars., *Pistacia terebinthus*, *Eugenia* vars., *Podocarpus macrophyllus*, *Olea europaea*, *Pinus halepensis*, *Nandina domestica*, *Serissa foetida*, *Juniperus californica*, *Punica granatum*, *Lagerstroemia indica*, *Bougainvillea* vars., *Crassula arborescens*, and some varieties of azalea.

Favourable temperatures

Sub-tropical trees come from cooler climates than tropical trees. If you consider the temperatures around the Mediterranean, then you will have a good idea of optimum temperatures for sub-tropical trees. During the summer it can be extremely hot, but in the winter temperatures drop quite radically, and most sub-tropical trees will not like very high winter temperatures. Keep them in a cooler room of your home.

Snow can also be experienced in Mediterranean regions in the winter. Although these trees in the wild will not appreciate very cold conditions, they are occasionally frosted. This does not mean, however, that the temperature where you keep your sub-tropical bonsai trees should fall much below 10° C (50° F). As a guide, it is suggested that sub-tropical

trees are kept at a temperature of between 8° C (46° F) and 22° C (72° F). They will also prefer the temperature to be a little lower during the night than it is during the day. But don't forget that draughty gap between a heavy curtain and a window (especially one that is not double glazed), which can be freezing during very cold nights. If the windowsill is the normal position of your bonsai during the day, then they should be moved away to a cool, but relatively protected, position during the night.

Although tropical trees can normally survive quite happily near a central-heating radiator, one should not place a collecton of sub-tropical trees too close to this intense source of heat. The best position for sub-tropical trees is in a comparatively cool part of the house that still receives enough warmth to keep them in good condition.

As a rule, sub-tropical trees need a certain amount of extra heat if they are to survive indoors in temperate climates during the winter.

Light levels and day length

Sub-tropical trees experience seasonal changes in both temperature and in day length. You will remember that on the equator day length and night length is exactly the same all the year round. The further away from the equator, towards either the North or South Pole, the greater the changes in day and night length as the seasons change. In the summer sub-tropical trees will experience longer days than tropical trees, and in the winter they will experience shorter days. As a general rule sub-tropical trees need slightly less intense light during the winter than tropical trees; but this should be watched closely and if the light level is not sufficient it should be supplemented by artificial lighting. Variegated trees and those with small leaves will require brighter conditions than other types.

A sign that your trees are not being given enough light is that the leaves will often turn pale. The lower leaves may also discolour and growth can be leggy, with extended gaps between leaves that are sometimes smaller than normal or, conversely, considerably larger as the plant searches for light, and tries to make as much use as possible of the little light that is available.

Trees that are exposed to too much light may have leaves that appear to be scorched. Light of too high an intensity can also produce the effect on your plant of not being given enough water. It follows that the dangers from too much intense light are not so damaging for sub-tropical trees, provided they have enough moisture.

Position

As with tropical trees, the position in which you keep

your collection of sub-tropical trees will be where the temperature and light levels described are best for them. We will assume that you have accepted the suggestion of making a permanent feature of your indoor bonsai, and that you have a collection that includes both tropical and sub-tropical trees. Sub-tropical trees will be happiest in the cooler part of your display, furthest away from any radiators but still with good light levels and well away from any cold draughts.

During the summer, after all danger of frost has passed, your sub-tropical trees can go outdoors to your outside display area, where they will benefit considerably from a rest period in the fresh air. But don't forget to bring them back into the warm well before danger of frost in the autumn.

Watering

The correct watering of sub-tropical trees is to all intents and purposes much the same as it is for tropical trees. The only difference, perhaps, is that during the winter, if your sub-tropical trees are being kept in a very warm atmosphere, they will need to be watered a little more in comparison to the summer months than would your tropical trees. The danger signs of either too little water or humidity, or too much, are the same as for tropical trees (see p.18).

Fertilizer

Fertilizer is also applied in the same way for sub-tropical trees, but it should be discontinued during the coldest months of the year, apart from maybe once every month or six weeks if needed. It should be recommenced when your trees start growing again.

Danger signs of either too much or too little fertilizer are the same as for tropical trees (see pp.19–20).

Holiday care

The same rules here as for tropical trees (see p.20).

Tender temperate trees

Among the varieties are some forms of *Fuchsia*, *Pyracantha*, *Buxus*, *Styrax*, *Camellia* and *Ficus carica*, (this is the fig that grows well outdoors in Europe), etc. Also included are all Japanese and normally hardy trees that are growing over rocks with their roots exposed; and trees that are growing or grown as Mame, and are in very small or shallow pots. During extended periods of frost normally hardy trees that are evergreen, especially broad-leaved evergreen, can

suffer severely. During frosts very old or weak trees, and those with very fleshy roots, should also be regarded as tender.

Temperatures, winter and summer

The reason for including the above mentioned trees in a book mainly devoted to those that can stay indoors – in fact have to be protected for much of the year – is that when the weather becomes excessively cold, these varieties can die or suffer severe die-back. You will be used to seeing a lot of these varieties growing around, either in gardens or in the neighbouring hedgerows and fields. It must be remembered that when planting a bonsai tree the roots cannot travel far underground and therefore have to be protected from the severest weather.

You will only need to protect these trees when it is extremely cold and frost persists for more than a few days. Put them in either a very cold room of the house that does not exceed 10° C (50° F), or in a greenhouse or similar structure. Most of these plants will not suffer by being kept relatively dark during their periods of protection from the frost, so a garden shed is also suitable. Use a thermostatically-controlled heater to stop the temperature going below freezing. Alternatively, in a small area the cost of running a simple fan heater occasionally will be negligible in comparison to saving your valued specimens.

During other seasons, or infrequent and slight frosts, these trees will not need protecting at all.

The needs of these temperate trees with regard to humidity, watering, feeding, and holiday care, etc., are the same as those for any other trees.

Light levels and day length

Light levels are of very little importance because during most of the time these trees will be outside and experiencing the light and day length that is natural to them. If and when they are actually brought into the home they should be displayed as far away as possible from any immediate source of heat, e.g. radiators and gas stoves. They should also be given as much light as possible, as well as placed in a draught-free position if they are inside during the summer months. During the winter light levels are of less importance if they are only being protected for short periods. However it must be remembered that they should be returned outside to their natural habitat as soon as possible after the danger of damage by frost has passed. This is not to say, of course, that they cannot be brought into the home for short periods during any other time, but they should not be treated as sub-tropical and tropical trees that need considerably more heat. Their dormancy should be interrupted as little as possible.

Temperate trees in sub-tropical and tropical regions

If you live in a hot region where the summer temperature is extremely high and winter temperature falls only a little – and certainly does not go down to freezing – then trying to grow temperate trees successfully in this area can be a problem. Like tropical and sub-tropical trees placed in a temperate climate, they have to be regarded as trees growing outside their normal habitat. You will have to try and reproduce as far as possible the temperatures and light levels which they are used to.

Favourable temperatures, winter and summer

Temperate trees are used to distinct seasons: spring, summer, autumn, and winter. During the winter these trees experience temperatures that go down to and sometimes lower than freezing point. In the summer the temperature does not normally go above that experienced by sub-tropical and tropical trees during their winter.

The most important thing to remember with temperate trees is that they have a dormant season when the top growth has ceased to grow and the roots are barely moving. During this period you will need to achieve temperatures of between 5°C (41°F) and 7°C (45°F), which can present considerable difficulties for those of you living in hot areas. In Australia, South Africa and Mediterranean-type regions most temperate trees will normally survive happily if their winter temperature does not exceed around 10°C (50°F). In hotter areas the bonsai enthusiast would need to install some form of air conditioning so that during the winter months (around three months) these trees may be kept at a cool temperature, no more than 10°C (50°F).

In localities where it is considerably hotter than temperate regions, it is necessary to keep temperate trees at a lower temperature than that experienced outside. During the summer months it will be possible to keep your trees outdoors, but they must still be kept in as cool and protected a position as possible, in shade and never allowed exposure to afternoon sunshine.

Light levels and day lengths

As previously discussed, tropical trees are used to light of a much higher intensity than those from temperate regions. During the hottest period of the year in sub-tropical and tropical regions, day length is in fact shorter than that experienced in temperate areas, but when the sun is out it is much stronger.

Temperate trees are encouraged to consider that it is time to start growing not just by a rise in temperature, but also by the increase in day length. It follows, therefore, that you will need to shorten the day length artificially in the winter months with the use of shading. During the summer, although the trees will need protecting from excessively strong sunlight, their day length could be extended by the use of supplementry lighting in the early morning and evening.

Position

If you can find a well protected spot outside during the summer your trees will be fine there for short periods. But again it is advisable to have a permanent display within your own home where you can recreate the right day length and cool temperatures that these particular trees need. As the air in tropical latitudes is considerably warmer than that in temperate regions, they will not suffer so much during the summer months from draughts, but in the winter when they should be dormant, warm draughts can mislead temperate trees into considering that it is time to start growing again.

Watering

In hot areas, although the rules for watering are still much the same as for tropical and sub-tropical specimens, your temperate trees will have to be looked at frequently to make sure that they do not dry out, particularly during the summer months. Spray the trees with water at least once a day.

Feeding

Feeding of temperate trees should only be carried out during the months they are actively in growth. If you cannot maintain a period of dormancy for as long as has been suggested, then start feeding gradually again immediately the tree starts to make new growth.

Holiday care

Trees in hot areas that are normally used to cool conditions can cause considerable difficulties when leaving them to go away on holiday. I would advise you to find somebody responsible to care for your trees, giving them all the help and instruction that you, through your own experience, have found to be the correct way to look after them. Remember that you can improve the humidity and water retention of your trees by putting them in plastic bags, or installing a drip watering system (see p.20).

CHAPTER 3

Styles of bonsai

Describing styles of bonsai is a way of classifying them. Some of these might appear to be somewhat pedantic, but it is felt that the bonsai enthusiast needs to know these especially if he or she has any intention of ever exhibiting them in flower shows, or bonsai club meetings.

Size

Trees less than 5 cm (2 in) high are called thimble bonsai. They can be extremely hard to look after, and time-consuming, because of the necessarily miniature size of the pot. Trees from 5–15 cm (2–6 in) are called Mame by the Japanese, but we can think of them as being miniature bonsai. Trees between 15 and 30 cm (6–12 in) are termed small bonsai. Those between 30 and 60 cm (12–24 in) are medium bonsai. Between 60 cm and 1.2 m (24–48 in) are the large bonsai. Those over 1.2 m (48 in) are called emperor bonsai trees. The last classification barely comes under the usual definition of bonsai, but trees of this height are often displayed in very large halls and gardens.

Classification of single trunk styles

This more or less describes the angle at which a single trunk stands in the pot.

Formal upright (Fig.10)
This style, as the name implies, is extremely formalized, with considerable rules as to the taper of the trunk and also the positioning of each and every branch. It is a style not so much in fashion today as growers are preferring to train their trees to look as natural as possible, emulating nature as it is and not as we think it should be.

Informal upright (Fig.11)
As the name suggests, this describes a tree that stands at a slight angle in the pot; the branch formation is not so formalized and it is one of the most popular styles used today. The angle at which

the trunk stands in the pot varies from the upright to approximately 30° from the vertical.

Slanting – windswept (Fig.12)
Here the style angles between 30 and 50° in the pot. As the name implies, it is a form of tree that you would see growing on an exposed moorland or near the sea.

Cascade (Fig.13)
This style grows from the horizontal to a tree that is cascading vertically downwards. The image created may be one of severe towering cliffs that are battered by the elements.

Semi-cascade (Fig.14)
This is a style that grows almost at the horizontal, accentuating the force of nature on growing trees.

Broom (Fig.15)
Broom style trees create a picture of deciduous trees growing in pleasant countryside. Their branches are always trained upwards.

   This style is only suitable for those indoor bonsai that have very small leaves.

Literati (Fig.16)
This style is particularly suitable for coniferous trees. It could be described as a very poetic style. The name literati is derived from the sort of calligraphy that Chinese and Japanese scholars are prone to execute – a free and cursive use of their brush in writing or painting. It is somewhat stylistic, and may not be suitable for many tropical trees.

Clump (Fig.17)
The next classification for bonsai trees is used for when more than one trunk is being produced from the same root. This can be a twin, three-, or even more than three-trunk tree, but it is not normal to grow an even number of trees such as four. The reason for this is that it is considered unlucky; and it is also difficult to balance a planting with a small

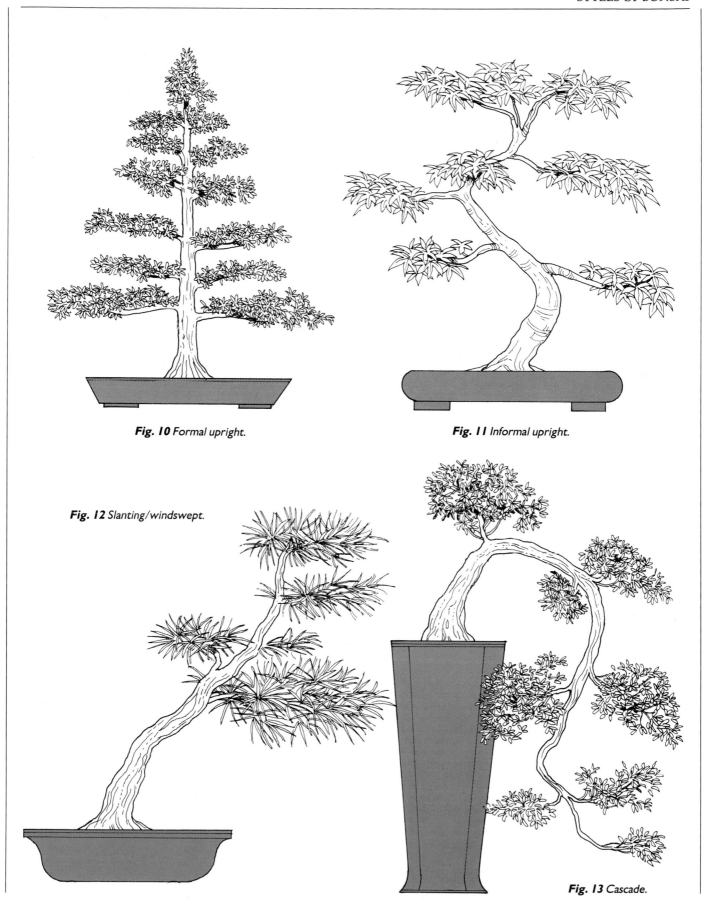

Fig. 10 *Formal upright.*

Fig. 11 *Informal upright.*

Fig. 12 *Slanting/windswept.*

Fig. 13 *Cascade.*

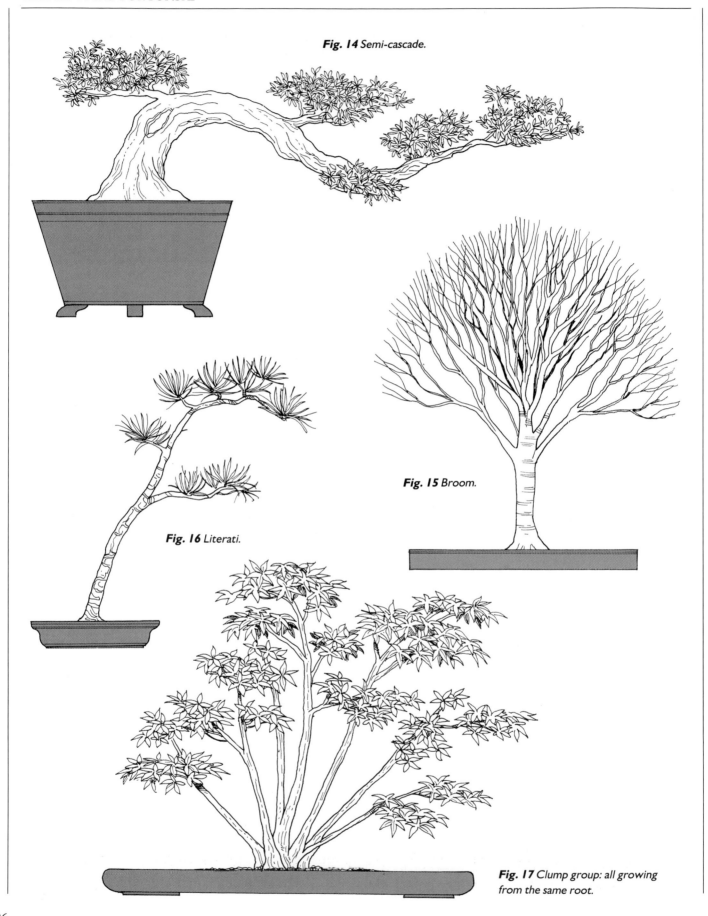

Fig. 14 Semi-cascade.

Fig. 15 Broom.

Fig. 16 Literati.

Fig. 17 Clump group: all growing from the same root.

group of evenly-numbered trunks or trees. Once beyond ten trunks, then really it does not matter whether or not the number of trunks are even. However the purist will disagree and the rules of bonsai say that no multiple-trunked group should have an even number of trunks.

Raft plantings (Fig.18)
A raft planting is where one tree has been laid down in a pot; the various branches are trained in one direction and after the tree has rooted throughout its length, these branches are trained as individual trees in their own right. They will thus become a group or forest planting, but as they are all connected it is termed a raft.

Groups (Figs.19a and b)
Groups can be trained as a raft; they can be planted individually, bearing in mind perspective, and thus forming a group or forest planting.

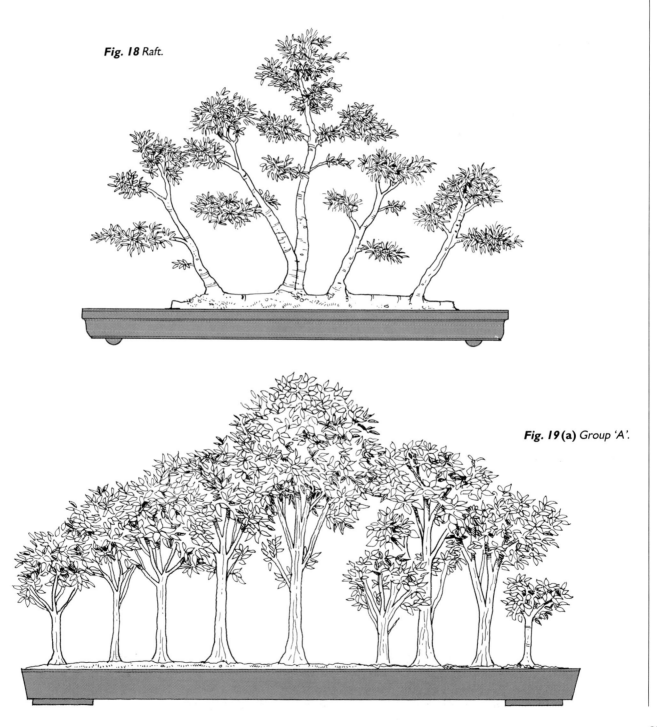

Fig. 18 Raft.

Fig. 19 (a) Group 'A'.

Fig. 19 (b) *Group 'B'.*

Fig. 20 *Root over rock.*

Fig. 21(a) *Saikei – One tiny tree in landscape.*

Fig. 21(b) *Saikei forest. These trays do not have drainage holes. Water can be added if desired.*

Rocks (Fig.20)

Rock plantings are considered a delight by many bonsai growers. He can use the rock either as a pot in itself, or the tree can be trained so that the roots grow down over the rock. The latter tends to remind one of the ancient temples in the tropics where trees have now taken over. Birds have left seeds upon the top of a ruin and slowly, as the trees have grown, the roots descend down the sides of the temple and over the years, gradually, encase it.

Landscapes (Fig.21a and b)

To the purist, small landscapes constructed of rock and miniature trees are not, strictly speaking, bonsai, but nonetheless pleasing effects can be made with a little imagination. These we will examine later.

CHAPTER 4

Propagation

As with other plants, trees, and shrubs, indoor bonsai trees can be propagated by the normal methods. They can be grown from seed, or, slightly quicker, they can be layered or air layered, divided, grafted or produced from cuttings.

Bonsai from seed

The one big advantage of growing tropical or sub-tropical bonsai trees from seed is that in the majority of cases these seeds do not need stratifying.

Stratifying is a process normally associated with trees that experience frost. It occurs as a form of protection to the tree seed. In the autumn the tree will shed its seed. This will then lie in the soil during the winter, where inevitably it will be exposed to frost. This exposure causes the hard outer layer of the seed to crack and weaken so that it becomes ready to germinate in the warmer weather of the spring. However this is not the case with sub-tropical or tropical seeds which, in their natural environment, experience little or no frost.

Sometimes it is necessary to use a slightly different method of softening shells of harder seeds, such as soaking the seed for at least 24 hours so that it absorbs water. They can be left longer than this with very little damage, but when you decide to plant them, any seeds that are left floating on the surface of the water should be discarded.

When you plant your seed, use a good quality seed compost and plant them to at least their own depth (Fig.22). If you are not certain which way up they should be then experiment. Plant some one way, and some the other. With seeds from the warmer climates, you will normally see germination fairly soon. If you have different varieties of seed, it is advisable to sow them in separate pots as some, especially those with thick hard shells, can take longer to germinate than others.

To encourage germination keep your seeds warm and dark until they start growing. Once they have germinated you should treat the whole pot with a fungicide that fights 'damping off', which can kill seedlings very easily. When your seedlings are large enough they should be transplanted, but do be very careful as this is a delicate operation – on no account should roots be damaged or pruned at this stage.

After being planted in larger pots your seedlings should be allowed to grow on for a year. If you fertilize well they will grow rapidly and, once strong enough, top pruning can be carried out. Unless it happens to be exceptionally strong, don't wire train your seedling during this period.

The illustrations show you the easy early stages of initial pruning.

Easy seeds for children

Children can be encouraged to show an interest in indoor bonsai, as well as ordinary plants, by planting some of the seed freely available when you buy fruit etc. Among those that are easy to grow are *Citrus* (lemon, grapefruit, orange, etc.), *Persea americana* (avocado), *Phoenix dactylifera* (date palm), *Punica granatum* (pomegranate), *Litchi chinensis* (lychee), *Pistacia* (pistachio), *Coffea arabica* (coffee). The above list is by no means complete, but it will give you a good idea of some of the varieties available. Your children (and you) will have enjoyment and education watching 'their' seeds grow; and on germination they can be treated in exactly the same way as any other seedling being converted to indoor bonsai trees.

Three alternative ways of dealing with the initial pruning of seedlings are shown in Figs.23–25.

A final point that should be noted is that the seeds used in planting trees that will become indoor bonsai are the same seeds as those used for that variety to be grown in any other way.

Cuttings

Cuttings can be taken from many tropical trees, and they will often root very easily. Exact varieties for which this method is recommended are described

Fig. 22 *Planting seed.*

Soil surface

Seed planted to its own depth

later in the detailed cultural notes on various trees.

Although cuttings can be made from small thinnings or prunings, it is advisable to have a cutting that is at least 10–15 cm (4–6 in) tall. The leaves should be stripped off, apart from two at the apex. The base should then be treated with a rooting hormone (Fig.26) and they should be inserted about one third of their length into a mixture of sharp sand and peat. Water well and, as they are tropical trees, they should be given adequate heat at the base. You can use either a heated tray or keep them in an airing cupboard or a greenhouse if it is available.

Fig. 23 *Initial pruning of seedlings: alternate leaves.*

a

b

c

Fig. 24 *Initial pruning of seedlings: alternate leaves – different method.*

a

b

c

Fig. 25 *Initial pruning of seedlings: opposite leaves.*

a

Remove including bud

b

c

Fig. 26 *Cuttings.*

Remove all lower leaves and buds

Remove half bark at the base

Rooting hormone

Cut at this angle

Air layering/layering

Although a lot of tropical trees will take readily from cuttings, you might have a specimen with a large branch that you would like to prune. This branch can become another bonsai tree in its own right.

If you wish to air layer then the branch should be ringed completely around twice. The bark between the incisions should be removed (Fig.27) – this gap will be between 2.5 and 4 cm (1–1½ in). The wound that you have created should be treated with a rooting hormone, and then covered with a material like damp sphagnum moss or wet peat. This should be packed out to at least twice the size of the potential trunk (Fig.28). It should then be covered completely with a film of clear plastic that is tied top and bottom. You will need to water the moss before covering it. After a number of weeks or maybe a couple of months, you will see white roots growing through the moss or peat. When these have begun to fill the 'container' or plastic that you have made, it is time to remove your new bonsai tree.

Direct layering is much the same as air layering, only in this particular instance you will bend a branch of the tree down to soil level. You will still remove a certain portion of the bark and insert this wounded portion in a pot or tray that contains compost. You will need to pin or tie the branch down, and after a certain length of time this branch will root itself into its new container.

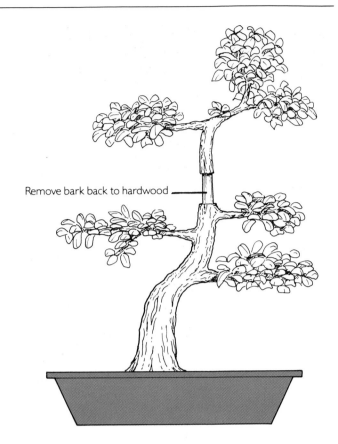

Remove bark back to hardwood

Fig. 27 *Air layering.*

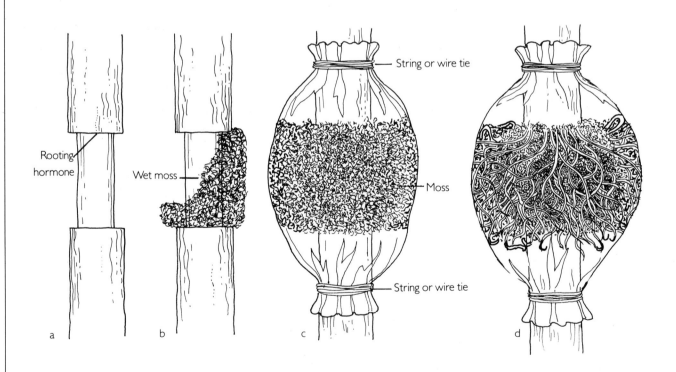

Rooting hormone

Wet moss

String or wire tie

Moss

String or wire tie

a   b   c   d

Fig. 28 *Air layering, continued.*

The ideal season to undertake direct layering or air layering is the spring, just before new growth appears. At this time the tree is becoming active and new roots will appear readily. You can attempt layering at other times of the year with varieties like ficus, that root readily. However, if you are not sure, then the early spring is the safest season.

An interesting point to note is that the circulation of sap within the trunk or an individual branch actually helps an air layering to root. A cross section of a tree will indicate this. The outermost layer that we see is the bark. Within this is a single cell layer of bark cambium, which continually forms new bark. Next comes a spongy layer called the phloem. As sap

(1) *An air layering showing rapid root growth after approximately three months.* (2) *Removing the rooted air layering.* (3) *Pot into a temporary pot without disturbing the roots.* (4) *The newly rooted 'tree' is now potted and securely tied in.*

flows back down the tree it feeds new wood cells that are forming all the time, as well as taking sugar nutrients down to feed the roots.

Although only one cell thick, the cambium layer is the most important part of the whole tree, producing cells for the sapwood on its innermost side, and on its outer side producing cells for the phloem. Without the cambium the tree would die.

Fig. 29 **Top grafting.** (a) *Stock with cut down centre; (b) Scion cut to a wedge shape at base; (c) Scion inserted into stock; (d) Side view; (e) Graft bound with raffia and then covered with grafting wax.*

Fig. 30 **Bud grafting.** (a) *Stock with 'T' cut. Bark peeled back; (b) Prepared bud with inner hard wood carefully removed; (c) Bud inserted; (d) Bark folded back over bud and secured with raffia or rose tie.*

Next comes the sapwood, through which sap travels up from the roots to the branches and leaves. It carries and stores nutrients as well as carrying them from one part of the tree to another. This is the part of the tree that forms the familiar 'rings'. The most active part of the sapwood is this year's growth or 'ring'. At the centre of the tree is the heartwood that, to all intents and purposes is dead.

As you see, sap travels up the inner part of the tree and back down to the roots through the phloem, which is on the outside of the tree. It follows from this that if you wound the tree by ringing it, as you do when air layering, then you do not affect the flow of the sap upwards. However, the *return* flow of the sap to the roots is interrupted. This means that energy sent up into the branch from the roots becomes contained within the air layering and does not just dissipate back to the roots. The 'new tree' continues to work naturally to feed the roots that it no longer has, and in so doing is then triggered to produce its own roots. These new roots eventually take over and are able to sustain the new tree.

This physiological need to root also indicates the reason why so many trees are able to be propagated by cuttings.

Grafting

Grafting is carried out with many temperate trees in the world of horticulture. Some trees can have fairly weak roots and their growth and strength can be improved by grafting a portion (scion) on to a stronger root system (stock) that comes from the same family of trees (Fig.29). This is especially true of flowering and fruiting trees in commercial nurseries, as well as some temperate bonsai that flower and fruit.

Grafting in the above manner is not used so often with tropical and sub-tropical trees. Nevertheless grafting can be used to 'implant' a branch where it is needed. If you are feeling very ambitious and wish to improve the base of a tree, you can also graft new roots.

Grafting can be roughly divided into three categories.

Bud grafting (Fig.30)
A bud is removed from a young but manageable size branch when the sap is flowing freely. This is normally just before mid summer. After making a 'T'-shaped cut to the sapwood on the tree to be grafted, the bud should be removed from its branch. After taking out the woody portion from the bud it should be inserted into the 'T' cut. The bark should be folded over the bud. It should then be bound with raffia and sealed with grafting wax. (If you know a friendly rose grower, perhaps he will let you have some 'rose ties' that tie in the bud and seal it in one easy operation.) Later that year or early next spring you will be able to see whether your bud graft has taken.

Top or side grafting (Fig.31)
There are many different ways of grafting in this manner. It can be used to graft a weaker tree to a stronger root stock. It can also be used to add branches where they are needed.

Basically one takes a portion of the wood to be grafted (scion). By shaving down one or two sides you reveal a portion of the cambium layer of the scion. These scions can be stored in damp cool sand until they are needed. In the late winter or early spring the bark of the stock is opened and the scion is inserted. It is absolutely essential that this is done so that the cambium of the scion is in as much direct contact with the cambium of the stock as possible; without this contact you cannot have a successful graft. The wound is then tightly bound with raffia and sealed with either grafting wax or a wound sealant that remains semi-liquid under the outer skin.

Root grafting (Fig.32)
Root grafting is much the same as top grafting. It should be done at the same time of the year. It might be necessary to lift the tree halfway out of the pot in order that the graft may be bound into position. To avoid disturbing the tree it is better if the new root can be kept in position by pinning it into the compost and sealing the wound as described before. If you choose the latter method then you have to be quite sure that the cambium layers are making good contact. You must also make sure that the tree is disturbed as little as possible during the time the graft takes to set.

Do make sure that both stock and scion are not damaged by disease, and that both are thoroughly clean. Lastly, do not forget that it is the contact between the two cambium layers that determines whether your graft is successful or not.

Fig. 31 **'Side' grafting.** (a) *Stock with bark peeled back;* (b) *Scions with one side shaved down;* (c) *Scions inserted into stock;* (d) *Graft bound with raffia and covered with grafting wax.*

Fig. 32 **Root grafting.** (a) *Looking down on the tree, this is a perfect root formation apart from 'A';* (b) *Position of insertion of new root;* (c) *Incision of bark;* (d) *Open flaps in bark and introduce new root;* (e) *Tightly seal root in position with raffia and graft sealing wax.*

CHAPTER 5

Training indoor bonsai

Pruning

When the novice bonsai enthusiast is faced with his or her first tasks of pruning, they tend to think of it as one of the 'Mysteries of the East' and completely beyond them. This is certainly not the case and with the application of a few simple rules, good quality pruning should be relatively simple.

There are two basic ways to think of pruning. The first is for the general health of the tree and the second is the more aesthetic pruning that is carried out to enhance and improve the appearance of the tree.

I might have detected a few raised eyebrows at the mention of pruning for the health of the tree. Nevertheless, this is a fact, as I shall explain. With trees growing in the wild their root growth is hardly restricted, except where trees are growing in a very rocky area. Under these circumstances roots travel as far as the tree needs, in order to gather the moisture and nutrients required to maintain the health of the more visible part of the tree. In fact Nature itself prunes the top of the tree: unwanted branches will die back and fall away; branches that are overcrowded and not receiving enough sunlight will also do the same; wind and snow will break other branches. But what about the *invisible* growth of the tree? In most cases the roots will grow at least as far underground sideways as does the top growth. However this is not the case with a bonsai tree.

Bonsai trees have their roots confined in a comparatively shallow and narrow pot. While the top growth grows to its utmost ability their roots can travel no further than the sides of the container. If this process is allowed to carry on, then the balance between the size of the root ball and the top growth will be destroyed. The roots work overtime to support the top, and if this is not pruned back, they become unable to do their job as efficiently as they would do normally. If this occurs the tree can suffer considerably and might even die from starvation. As a rough guide, the area of the pot or root ball for a bonsai tree is approximately a quarter to one-third of that taken up by the trunk, branches and leaves, etc. As this is the case, the top growth of your tree will need to be pruned throughout the growing season, simply to maintain the health of your tree as well as improving its shape.

For trees that experience seasonal changes in temperature and day lengths, then pruning tends to be divided into two phases. Heavy branch pruning (Fig.33), where one is removing larger branches, is often left until the dormant season, when it is easier, in the case of deciduous trees, to see what one is doing. Also the sap is not flowing, so you do not have to worry about the tree weeping through the pruning wounds that you produce. Pruning new growth as well as leaf pruning is carried out with temperate trees during the growing season.

With trees that originate in tropical and sub-tropical regions, pruning is not so divided. Generally speaking, both heavy branch pruning as well as general pruning can be carried out throughout the year. The reason for this is that these trees do not experience such a disruption in their growth as do temperate trees. Although they have a shortish dormant period, when their growth is considerably diminished, it is certainly not to the same extent as that experienced by temperate trees.

Incidentally, do not fall into the trap of thinking that because you have bought an old mature bonsai that it will not need pruning. *All* bonsai need pruning throughout their life. If your tree does not need pruning it is dead!

Let us imagine that in front of you is your recently acquired tree. You might even have started to experiment with pruning on a houseplant. There is nothing wrong with this and it can help you learn the techniques (Fig.34). Remember all pruning that you do will combine the two aims of maintaining the health of your tree and increasing its beauty.

You are now an artist with brushes and paints, and in front of you is your canvas. It already has the outline of the tree that you wish to create. Now I can begin to tell you of the more obvious parts of your tree that need pruning.

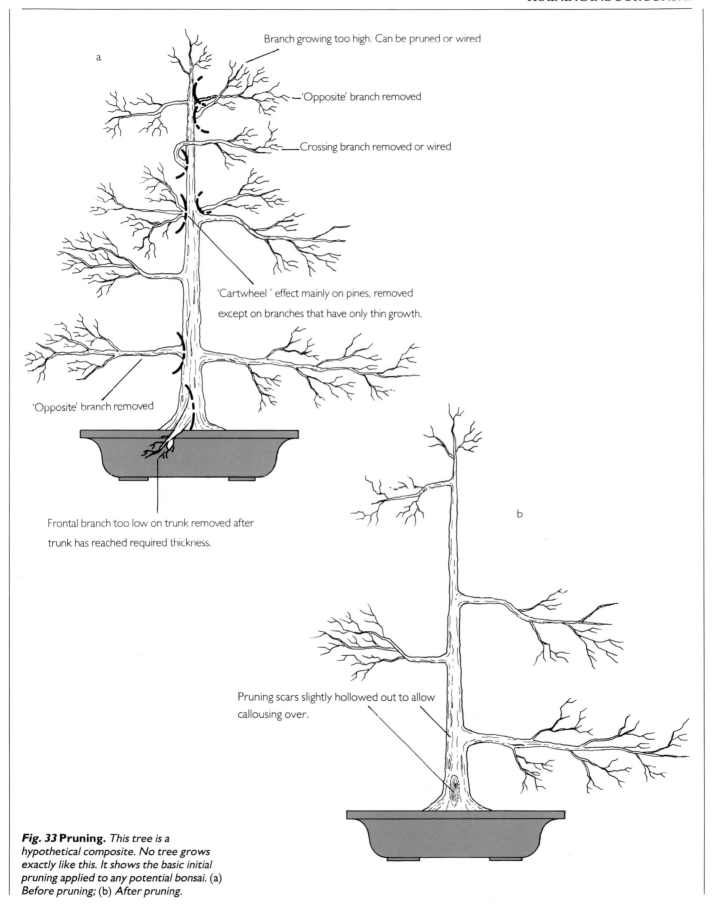

Branch growing too high. Can be pruned or wired

'Opposite' branch removed

Crossing branch removed or wired

'Cartwheel ' effect mainly on pines, removed except on branches that have only thin growth.

'Opposite' branch removed

Frontal branch too low on trunk removed after trunk has reached required thickness.

Pruning scars slightly hollowed out to allow callousing over.

Fig. 33 Pruning. *This tree is a hypothetical composite. No tree grows exactly like this. It shows the basic initial pruning applied to any potential bonsai. (a) Before pruning; (b) After pruning.*

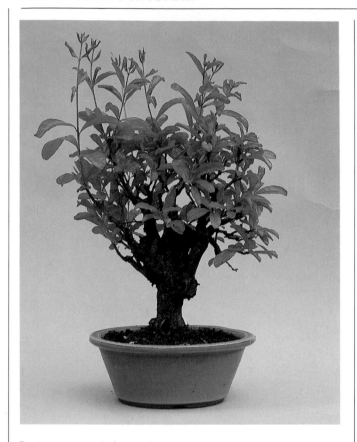

Punica granatum before spring pruning.

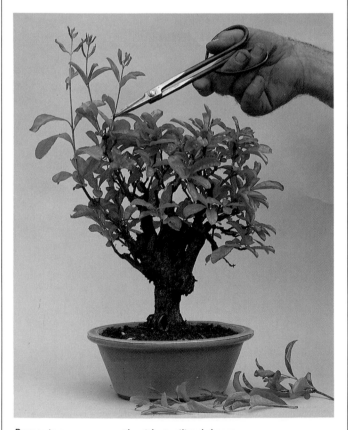

Removing excess growth with sterilized shears.

Leaf pruning

Certain varieties of both temperate as well as tropical and sub-tropical trees can be leaf pruned around two months after new growth starts in the spring. Leaf pruning (Fig.35) should only be done on trees that are growing healthily, and are not too old. With older trees, and ones that are somewhat suspect in their health, only remove such leaves that appear to be too large for the tree as a whole.

Temperate trees for which this procedure is employed include acers (maples), zelkovas (grey bark elm), *Fagus* (beech), and *Ulmus* (elms), etc. Amongst the tropical and sub-tropical trees we could include *Ulmus* (elms), zelkovas (grey bark elm), *Sterculia rupestris* (bottle tree) and *Ficus* (fig) varieties. As a general rule, flowering trees should not be leaf pruned, but over-large leaves can be removed. Evergreen needle trees such as pines, junipers, etc., cannot be leaf pruned.

To leaf prune, one should cut the whole of the leaf off, leaving just the leaf petiole. The petiole is the stalk of the leaf. After a number of weeks this petiole will wither and fall. The new buds that were dormant up to the time you removed the leaf will now take over, opening to form leaves and shoots. The advantage of this technique is to produce smaller leaves and a finer more twiggy outline to the tree. With deciduous trees it will help to produce a better autumn colour. The tree is also producing almost two years' growth in one season: do make sure that the tree is in first-class condition, and that it has been well fertilized up to the time of leaf pruning.

General pruning

One of the disadvantages of heavy pruning is that it can scar a trunk or branch. In order to encourage the tree to callous over this wound and to stop the entry of fungal diseases, it is advisable to seal the wound you have created by pruning. Sealing compounds are now available that do not go hard after being applied to the wound. They form a skin and underneath that skin the compound remains comparatively liquid; thus when the tree expands or contracts in growth during colder or warmer weather, the sealing compound will expand and contract with the tree. As hard sealers are not flexible, they tend to crack after a relatively short time, allowing the entry of disease and insects that you have tried hard to keep out.

It should be noted that some horticulturists now question the beneficial effects of a sealing compound but I believe the use of a flexible sealant is efficacious.

With heavy branch pruning initial scarring is inevitable, but the tree will eventually heal over. One way to induce callousing quickly is to trim the severed bark with a razor-edge knife. This induces the wound to cover over rapidly, thus adding to the aged look of the trunk or large branch.

Fig. 34 *Deciduous branch pruning.*

(a) *Cut branch above first or second leaf;*

Prune here for higher branch

(b) *Growth after pruning.*

Prune here for lower branch

Fig. 35 *Leaf pruning.*

Dormant buds in leaf axils

Cut off leaf, leaving leaf petiole

Leaf petiole or stalk

Normal pruning

Fig. 36 Bud Pruning.

Bud pruning

(a) *Before.*

(b) *Three months later.*

Fig. 37 Evergreen branch pruning

(a) **Pine pruning.** *Entirely remove centre 'candle'. Prune back other 'candles' by at least one-half. Break by twisting, or cut, being careful not to cut needle.*

(b) **Aleppo pine.** *Prune by either pinching or cutting back to small dormant bud. Be careful to avoid cutting through needles.*

New growth that has hardened off. This should be cut

(c) **Junipers and other conifers with segmented leaves.** *Ends should be pinched out to encourage bushy habit. Do not cut as you will cut across segments; cutting them will make them go brown.*

Bud pruning

One way to cut down on pruning during the growing season is to bud prune (Fig.36) before the buds actually open to form leaves and twigs. Your tree should be closely examined before new buds open so that you can determine the shape you wish your tree to be during the summer. When you have done this you will find that you have a number of extraneous buds which can be removed. This can be done with tweezers or fingers, or even a sharp knife or fine pair of scissors.

Bud removal will cut down the necessity for excessive pruning later in the year and it will conserve the energy in the tree for those buds that you wish to retain.

Perhaps the most important point about pruning is where you actually cut. With most broad-leaved trees allow them to develop four or five sets of leaves or, if they are alternate leaves, then allow four or five individual leaves. The base of this new growth will then have obtained a reasonable thickness. You can now prune back to one or two leaves. This is a general rule and where you want a branch to thicken rapidly then do not prune back as far as this. On the other hand there is nothing to prevent you pruning back deciduous trees considerably further than the present season's growth. Nevertheless, to be on the safe side, do not prune back further than a potential growth point.

When pruning back to the first or second leaf, it is as well to remember in which direction you wish the new growth to grow. If you prune back to a bud that points downwards, the new growth will tend to grow in that direction. This is the same for buds that point upwards. But with most trees their natural habit is to grow upwards, and the bud that is pointing upwards will tend to throw new growth at a steeper upward angle than the angle produced by a bud that is growing downwards.

Most tropical and sub-tropical trees are of broad-leaved varieties, but there are some evergreen needle trees such as *Pinus* (pines) and *Juniperus* (junipers). Most pines (Figs.37a and b), should be pruned in the spring by shortening, by about two-thirds, any new candles. With *Pinus halepensis* we have a pine that will retain its small needled, immature growth, provided it is pruned in the following way. This pine is unusual in as much that it has tiny dormant buds at the base of some of its needles, in the same manner as a tree like a *Juniperus* (juniper) (Fig.37c). As with many other needled trees like *Abies* etc., *Pinus halepensis* is pruned by finger pruning. This is done by gently holding the branch to be pruned in one hand, and twist pulling the section of needles on a branch to be pruned. The harder the growth, the more difficult this will be, but provided it is done when this new growth is a light green it is a very simple operation. Nevertheless one should be careful not to tear across needles, but rather leave them intact.

Once again let me reiterate that you should pause before commencing to prune. Be fully aware of what you are doing because once started there is no turning back. Once you have removed a branch, it is only time that will renew it, so if you make a mistake it is a long time before it can be rectified.

Experiment by placing pieces of paper around twigs and branches, so that you will see roughly the effect it will have when you do finally take the scissors in your hand and start pruning.

Wiring

You will continue training your bonsai tree by pruning, but on occasions wiring the tree to the desired shape is quicker and more effective. A semi mature tree or shrub can be obtained from garden centres or shops and within a period of only a few weeks or months, be transformed into a very satisfactory bonsai. If you try to do this simply by pruning you would need the patience of a saint, because it could take years. On the other hand, by gently training the whole tree with wire, this effect is achieved in a comparatively short time.

The bonsai enthusiast will normally use either copper wire, or anodized aluminium wire. Other wire can be employed for the same purpose, but there are disadvantages. Garden or electrical wire that is covered in brightly coloured plastic is distracting to say the least and, as the tree will remain wired for a number of months, is only acceptable aesthetically if nothing else is available.

Wire comes in various thicknesses and, generally

(1) *A two year old Ficus 'starlight' before wiring.* (2) *Wiring completed.* (3) *After wiring superfluous growth is removed.* (4) *Ficus wired, pruned and potted. The character of the original seedling has been completely altered.*

Fig. 38 *Other methods of training branches.*

Strings attached to trunk or branches

By weights

Strings or wire attached to pot

Supporting wire

Fig. 39 *Using a clamp to bend back a trunk to the position required.*

Fig. 40 *Windswept-style tree being trained to shape with use of a strong metal bar. This is tied securely where necessary. Pads of rubber should be placed under the wires to secure the bar to the tree.*

speaking, wire between thicknesses of 12 and 20 gauge could be considered the most useful. The lower the number, i.e. 12, the thicker the wire will be.

The advantage of anodized aluminium wire, which is not always readily available, is that it is softer than copper and does not normally need heating to make it more pliable. Like copper wire, it can be saved and used again and again. The disadvantage of aluminium wire is that, as it is softer than copper, a thicker grade of wire will be needed to achieve the same effect. The other disadvantage is in its colour. If this is brown then it will blend in reasonably well with the colour of your tree. However, if it is the natural aluminium colour you will have to put up with this throughout the training period.

The advantage of copper wire is that it is less

distracting. I have already mentioned that you will need less of it than aluminium wire to achieve the same effect; it will also blend better with the colour of the trunk and the branches of your tree, especially over a period of time when exposure to damp conditions softens its natural colour still further. The disadvantages of copper are that it will sometimes have to be heated in a wood shaving or paper fire to anneal it. This process softens the copper wire and makes it more pliable. Other lesser disadvantages are that it can sometimes rust and form a verdigris which can stain the trunk of the tree; and that it conducts heat and cold very easily so that during the winter the cold air can be accentuated around the tree.

Although one can use iron or steel wire, these are particularly difficult to work with because they do not bend easily. They also have the disadvantage of rusting and marking the trunk of your tree. I would advise against the use of iron wire if at all possible.

Other methods of training
Apart from wire, other ways can be used to bend the branches of your tree. Weights, for instance, can be suspended from various points along the branches (Fig.38), although the drawback here is that it takes a long time to achieve the desired effect. It is also not as precise as wiring in forming the shape required. If your tree is being kept outside during the summer, then be careful to protect it from high winds, as weights can easily damage the trunk and other branches by swinging against them.

Another method of bending is to tie strings to various points on the branches and anchor them to wires tied across the pot or even to other branches or the trunk itself. This method is also not as accurate as wiring the branches directly. Where one has a tightly forked branch, then a small piece of wood that had been carved out at either end can be inserted to open up this gap so that it looks more natural.

With very heavy and thick trunks or branches, wiring is not used. In this case clamps (jacks) are employed (Fig.39) These clamps have the advantage that the shape you want does not have to be forced on the tree all at once. They can be tightened or loosened gradually over a number of months. These clamps can also be used in conjunction with shaped or straight strong iron or steel bars (Fig.40).

Wire application

Whatever part of the tree is to be wired, one end of the wire will have to be securely anchored. If this is not done then the wire will not perform the job for which it is being applied. To determine the thickness of the wire needed, grasp the branch between your two hands and very gently test the tension by bending it up and down. The tension of the wire (Fig.41) will need to be slightly more than that of the branch itself. In some instances you will need to use two wires of the same diameter in order to bend and secure the branch in position.

Before you start wiring your first bonsai tree, it is a good idea to practise on a less prized specimen such as a shrub in your garden, or an indoor houseplant. By spending a little time feeling the tension of wire and branch and by experimenting with applying the wire, you will soon find that by following a few simple rules you will be able to shape trees to your full satisfaction.

Before you attempt to wire a full tree, gain some experience by wiring up a few small branches. When you have mastered this, and have created enough tension as well as putting the wire on at the right angle, you will be ready to try a full tree.

It is often found unnecessary to wire the trunk of any but the youngest trees. They have normally reached their required shape after only a few years. Nevertheless if you do need to wire the full tree you should proceed as follows.

Start with the thickest part of the tree and work towards the thinner branches and twigs. This means that you will wire the trunk first (Fig. 42). You should push your wire as deep into the soil as you can, keeping it as close to the trunk as possible. You should then coil the wire – not too tightly, but on the other hand not loosely – at approximately 45° angles up the length of the trunk. If the trunk of your tree becomes more flexible towards the top (i.e. thinner) then the heavy wire that you started with will need to be replaced with a slightly lighter wire the higher up the trunk you go. If this is the case then this second wire should be anchored underneath one of the coils of the first wire. (You can also accomplish this by wiring not just the top of the trunk of the tree, but also one of the branches at the same time.)

Fig. 41 Wiring. *First test the tension of both branch and wire to determine which wire to use.*

When the wire is in position on the trunk, you should then gently bend the trunk to its desired shape. As wiring is normally carried out on indoor trees when they are growing, it can be done at most times of the year; the sap will be flowing strongly, especially during the summer months.

When bending the trunk do it in stages, working your way up, and starting again at the bottom, so that it is being bent gently and slowly. Do not expect a living tree to be able to have its form changed by 45° immediately: in all but the strongest and most pliable trees this would mean that the trunk or branch would break. It is also inadvisable to wire trees after dusk as the flow of sap slows in the evening and they are likely to snap more easily.

When you have shaped the trunk to your satisfaction you can go on to the branches. Again you start with the thickest branches, which will be the lower ones of your tree. After you have wired the branches you progress to the smaller twigs. Very new soft growth is normally too flexible to wire satisfactorily, and you should wait until it has achieved a certain woodiness.

When you are wiring branches, be careful not to lay the wire over smaller branches or twigs coming off the branch, or even over leaves. When you come to the end of the branch the wire should be cut off and the last 12 mm (½ in) or so bent back loosely over the branch in order to stop it uncoiling itself.

After shaping the branches you will find that some small offshoot branches might now be bending in unfavourable directions. If this is the case, they can be either removed altogether, or wired to the shape and direction that the form of the tree and your imagination have dictated. A seedling or young tree, initially somewhat uninteresting, can be trained in a number of styles, including 'cascade' as shown in Fig.43.

After wiring, the active cells in the bark of the tree will have become altered, being either compressed or stretched to some extent. This will mean that your bonsai will need a certain length of time to recover, so for a couple of weeks or so try to keep the tree out of harsh direct sunlight and very windy conditions. It should also be sprayed over fairly regularly, and not fertilized for about a month.

Needless to say wiring puts some strain on the tree, and it should not be root pruned and repotted at the time, but normal top pruning can and should be carried out.

Fig. 42 **Wiring.** *To create an informal upright bonsai.*
(a) *Tree before wiring.*
(b) *After wiring.*
(c) *After the tree is wired, it is gradually and very carefully bent to the required shape.*

One wire used for two branches

Single wire anchored under trunk wire

First trunk wire ends

Lower wires anchored in soil

a

b

New deeper pot to suit and balance cascade style

Fig. 43 Creating a cascade tree.
First the tree is potted into a new pot, but angled over as far as possible. After settling and main pruning, the trunk is gradually bent over to the required angle. It must be stressed that with all but the youngest and most pliable trees, shaping to this acute angle should not be done all at once. It should be achieved over a number of days, if not weeks. (a) The young, untrained tree; (b) After the initial wiring and pruning. Within time this tree can achieve a very natural and aged look.

CHAPTER 6

Repotting indoor bonsai

Over the years the process of repotting a bonsai tree has continued to be a mystery to the uninitiated. A stranger to the cultivation of bonsai trees invariably says that, 'Oh yes, it is a process of cutting the roots, isn't it?' If only it was: all of the pruning and shaping would then not be necessary.

However pruning the roots does rejuvenate the tree: it actually makes the tree grow at a faster rate. Pruning the roots of a bonsai is especially important because, contained as it is in a small pot, it soon becomes pot bound with little or no nourishment left in the compost, and needs then to be repotted. Being pot bound can be dangerous for any plant: the more roots that are contained in a pot, the less compost there is for those roots to draw nutrients from.

As you prune the top growth almost continuously throughout the life of a bonsai, then occasionally the roots will need to be pruned as well. This maintains a balance between the top growth and the root growth. The reason that pruning roots rejuvenates growth is that the nearer the feeding roots (ciliary hairs) are to the main trunk of the tree, the quicker the tree will be able to absorb moisture and nutrients from the compost in which it is growing.

When to repot

Indications that the tree is ready for repotting are that you will see roots appearing through the drainage holes at the bottom of the pot. In extreme cases you will also be able to see roots starting to appear at the top of the pot, coiling around the edges of the compost next to the pot. Do not confuse these thin roots with the old ones growing at the base of the tree.

With any plants in this condition you have two alternatives. With most houseplants that are being grown in plastic or ornamental ceramic containers, then the normal course is to 'pot them on'. This entails removing the plant from its container and potting it on into a larger container to which can be added further supplies of fresh compost. With a bonsai tree, unless you wish it to be a larger specimen

– in which case it will also go into a larger pot – you will repot it into its original container. To do this, and to be able to add fresh clean compost, it becomes necessary for the roots of bonsai trees to be pruned.

Trees grown in temperate regions are invariably repotted and root pruned during their dormant season, i.e. during the colder months of the year, and about four to five weeks before the spring growth becomes evident. Most sub-tropical trees are also repotted during the coldest time of the year. Their dormancy period is not as long as for temperate trees, but it is much safer to root prune them when they are in less active growth than usual. Tropical trees can be repotted at almost any time of the year, and more safely than either sub-tropical or temperate trees; however I am of the opinion that it is still safer, even with tropical trees, to do this at the same time as sub-tropical and temperate trees.

To make absolutely sure your tree does need repotting, tap it gently around the sides of the pot and, holding it upside down, remove the pot from the root ball. If, whilst you are doing this, large pieces of soil start falling out, then you will know the tree does not need repotting. However, if having removed the pot the root ball is an almost solid mass of roots, then it definitely does need repotting.

Preparing for repotting

Before you start repotting, gather together all the tools that you will need. When deciding what compost to use, it should be borne in mind that bonsai trees are normally in fairly shallow pots. As this is the case, soil-free composts are not suitable; they will not hold the tree down firmly enough.

All composts serve a number of purposes. Firstly, they must be able to anchor a tree successfully so that the wind – or a passing cat, for that matter – does not easily knock it from its container. Secondly, the compost must be able to retain water but not to the extent that it remains sodden for long periods. Thirdly, and very importantly, the roots of trees need contact with the air, so composts that pack down too

Ready to repot. It is important to have everything you need close at hand before starting to repot. The pot is clean and dry. Drainage gravel, mesh for the drainage holes, as well as wire to tie the tree in, are all prepared.

hard are unsuitable. Because of this need for air circulation, it is suggested that if you use a mixture of bagged compost with sharp sand and peat, you take the trouble to sieve both the sand and the compost itself, to remove most of the very tiny particles that can sometimes clog the compost. One can also purchase ready-made bonsai compost from specialist nurseries as well as some garden centres. Although this compost is ideal for all general trees, if you have bonsai in your collection that you feel need more or less drainage, then you can add sharp sand or grit.

If you are feeling particularly energetic, you may wish to make up your own compost for your trees. However, if you do this, please remember the purposes that a compost must serve: holding the tree, retention of water and fertilizer, and allowing proper drainage and aeration around the root ball.

Composts

Most composts used for bonsai trees will have loam as their main constituent. You can use loam dug from your garden, but it will have to be sterilized, and also tested for PH factor as well as the presence of other essential chemical ingredients. If these are found to be lacking they will have to be added.

To avoid this, it is suggested that you buy ready-bagged composts and use them as a base for your own mixture. I would suggest the ideal compost to use would be something like John Innes No. 2, or its equivalent. This already contains fertilizer which the tree will need for at least a few weeks, if not a couple of months, after being repotted. After this has leached from the pot you will need to add fertilizer.

You will also need a quantity of sterilized sharp grit and very sharp sand. (It might be worth mentioning in this context, that sharp means irregular pieces of both sand and grit.)

The compost or loam, as well as the sharp sand and grit, should now be sieved, the idea being to remove all the finer particles that might block drainage and

(1) *Wire has been inserted through drainage holes to tie the tree in. Drainage grit and compost prepared.* (2) *Tease out the roots and prune by approximately one third.* (3) *After putting in drainage grit and a thin layer of compost the tree should be introduced to the pot.* (4) *The tree has been tied in. The compost is carefully worked in around the root ball and the potting is completed after watering.*

interrupt aeration.

It must be remembered that you are trying to reproduce the natural growing conditions of each tree. As this is the case, compost can vary slightly for tropical and sub-tropical trees, bearing in mind the region in which they are grown. A good general purpose compost for sub-tropical and tropical trees would be as follows: five parts of loam (sieved), one part of grit (sieved), two parts of sharp sand (sieved), and two parts of peat. This mixture can be slightly altered for different varieties. Those that require more drainage should have less peat and more sand and grit added, and those that are used to damper conditions should have less grit and sand, and more peat or loam.

The process of repotting

After making your preparations, you are ready for the task of repotting (Fig.44). First of all you must remove the tree from the pot. Normally this is quite easy, by simply tapping around the sides of the pot and gently easing the tree out. Occasionally, if the tree is heavily rootbound, or if the pot is narrower at the top than it is in the middle, you will have to use a sharp sterilized knife to cut around the edges of the root ball in order that it might be removed. Place your tree on a turntable and gently start teasing out the roots with either a sharp stick or even a 15 cm (6 in) nail. You should be aiming to remove approximately

Fig. 44 Repotting

(a) Check whether tree needs repotting – an obvious sign would be roots protruding from the drainage holes.

(b) Take tree out of pot. Root ball is congested, so the tree needs repotting.

(c) After teasing out, you will be cutting off one-quarter to one-third of the root ball.

(d) Cover drainage holes with plastic net.

(e) Insert wire or string to retain root ball, if necessary.

(f) Cover bottom of pot with sterilized grit.

(g) Re-introduce tree. Tie in and add compost, making sure you fill all holes.

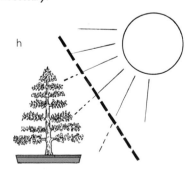
(h) After repotting, protect from excessive sunshine.

(i) Change the angle of the tree to the pot at this stage, if this is felt necessary. Finally, water thoroughly.

one-third of the root ball from around the sides and also from underneath. Tease the roots out slightly further than where you intend to prune them; it is advantageous to the tree to leave it with a small beard of roots that can easily penetrate the new compost.

Having carefully teased out just over one-third of the root ball you might be surprised by the length of the roots that will now be hanging down. Using a sharp pair of sterilized root pruners, or strong scissors, you should now cut off one-third of the original root ball, leaving the small beard of roots. After throroughly scrubbing out the pot, you must now decide whether it will hold the tree without wiring the root ball in.

Wiring in

You can easily determine whether your tree needs wiring in. A tall tree in a very small pot will almost certainly need to be wired in. A tree with a poor root structure and a root ball that is not fairly solid after you have root pruned it, will also need to be wired or secured into the pot.

If you feel that this is needed, then you can use wire if you feel the wire is likely to stay in place throughout the next few seasons' growth. But it can be difficult, on next repotting, to remove the old wire from the root ball. If the support will only be essential for a few months, then I suggest that you use a good quality string. This will break down and disappear after a time, and has the advantage that it will not interfere with the root growth in any way.

If it is considered necessary to either wire or string the root ball down, this should now be inserted through the drainage holes of the bonsai container, leaving both ends fairly long, so that they can be tied down easily. Small pieces of plastic mesh should be cut and laid over the drainage holes with the wire going through them. A layer of sterilized gravel or grit should now be scattered over the bottom of the pot to facilitate drainage and air circulation after the tree has been repotted. In very shallow trays only a small amount of grit will be necessary. Place a thin layer of your selected sieved compost over the grit. You are now ready to reintroduce the tree to its container. Carefully position the tree within its pot. Before you tie it in or add further compost be sure that it is in the right position to give the most pleasing effect. This should not necessarily be directly in the middle of the pot. For instance trees with longer branches on one side will need that side to sit further away from the side of the pot, in order that the overall effect is balanced.

Your tree will look natural and balanced when looked at from the front. From this angle the lower half of the trunk will have no branches growing towards you. Longer branches will be growing towards either side of the tree and it will have shorter branches at the back. It is only as branches become shorter and closer together, near the top of the tree, that a few small branches can be trained towards the front. The tree will often incline slightly forwards. With groups, the principal tree will always be positioned near the front of the group. Invariably the smaller trees are planted at the back of groups.

If you have considered it necessary to tie the tree into the pot, this should now be done. Try to hide the wire or string underneath some of the more prominent upper or surface roots. This will also stop the roots becoming damaged by the wire. After this has been done the majority of the compost can be added, firmed down as you go, and making sure that all small pockets in the root ball are filled with compost. You can do this either with a blunt stick if the compost is dampish, or with your finger tips. If you use your thumbs, the pressure you can put on the compost can be excessive and it might pack down too hard. The compost should not completely fill the container; you should leave it slightly below the rim. This will enable you to water your tree more easily in the subsequent months. It should be noted that the compost at the base of the trunk will be higher than that by the edges of the container. In other words it slopes down from the tree to the sides of the pot. When viewed at eye level this gives a pleasing and realistic effect to the newly planted tree.

Brush off all excess compost and snip off very fine roots that are protruding above the surface of the compost or, if you prefer, pin them down back into the compost. When you have done this sprinklings of fine gravel, small rocks, or moss etc. can be used to make the compost surface look more natural and undisturbed.

Now thoroughly water the repotted tree using the fine 'rose' of a watering can or, alternatively, placing it in a bowl of temperature-adjusted water and allowing the root ball to soak up the moisture. If the tree has not been tied into its pot you will have to be careful that water entering from the bottom does not lift the tree out again. After this has been completed you will need to protect your tree for a number of weeks from strong sunshine and heavy rain (if outside). It should not be fertilized during this period, and watering should be kept to a minimum, bearing in mind that the root ball has been weakened. Only water when the top layer of compost is becoming dry, although it will help the tree if you carefully spray its leaves more frequently than usual for a number of weeks.

Containers

If we accept the definition of the word bonsai as a plant in a container then you can see that the container is, in fact, an integral part of the life of the bonsai. Containers should be chosen with care to suit the style and type of tree that is going to be planted.

There are certain rules governing all containers. All pots will have at least one drainage hole to allow excess water to pass through, and also to allow the pot to be immersed in water so that the tree can be

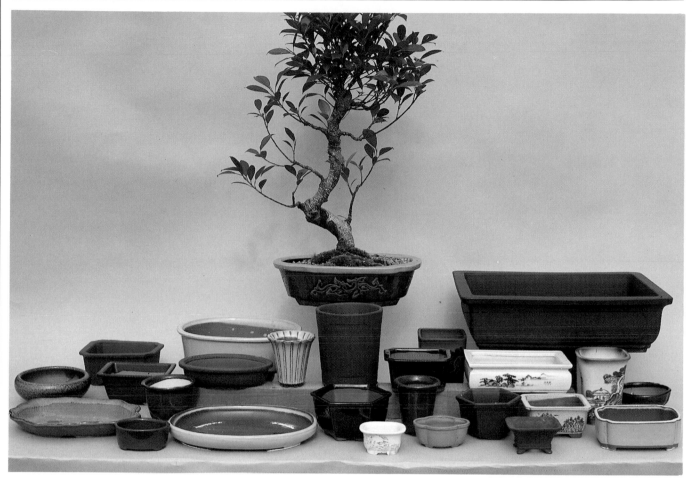

A selection of pots and containers showing some of the many styles, sizes and colours.

thoroughly watered. Most bonsai containers should not be glazed on the inside. If they are then this will remove the porosity of the pots, and the roots will be able to find little firm anchorage. Pots can be made out of a variety of materials, including the more common ceramic or clay pots. Others can be homemade from wood, carved out of stone, or can simply be a single slab of stone. They can also be an almost infinite number of shapes and patterns. Their size can vary from tiny 2–3 cm (¾–1¼ in) thimble pots to those designed to grow emperor bonsai that can be over a metre in length.

The colour container you choose should be one that will match and show off the tree; it should not detract too much from the plant itself. In Japan the more traditional bonsai pots are very rarely decorated with pictures or raised motives. Nevertheless, one can purchase containers made in, say, Taiwan, China or Thailand that are considerably more decorative. Many of the latter will have pictures of flowers, leaves, and such like, that have been painted on or raised to be fairly prominent on the sides of the pot. You should also choose a type of pot that you think you can live with for a number of years: after all, the tree will stay in your chosen container for quite a long

time. The choice of pot for a particular tree is up to the individual. In Japan pots tend to be considerably less deep than those chosen in China. For the Japanese a great deal of importance is made of the fine branches and leaves of a tree as well as the trunk. In China this is often not the case; and, in fact, Chinese trees sometimes look slightly odd to the Western eye which may be more accustomed to the style developed in a country like Japan. This is not to denigrate the way the Chinese train their trees, but you will often see a form with excessive trunk and little foliage and small twigs.

Different ways of growing trees occur in country after country and will greatly influence the choice of pot. To help you decide, and as an approximate guide, you will remember that the area of the pot, looking at it from eye level, is approximately a quarter to one-third that of the area taken up by the whole of the rest of the tree i.e. trunk, branches, and foliage. For heavy-trunked coniferous trees plain dark brown, fairly deep and rectangular pots are highly suitable. On the other hand trees that cascade should always have a deep pot, whether square or round. Groups of trees will normally be planted in shallow rectangular or oval pots.

CHAPTER 7

Special effects

Forest groups

A magnificent tree in a pot will give you considerable pleasure and satisfaction. Nevertheless you may have admired the forest groups in other people's collections. By creating one yourself, you will add a further dimension to your own collection of trees.

Worthwhile and attractive groups can be made fairly quickly, and relatively inexpensively. Generally speaking the main trees used in groups are fairly straight in growth, and not dramatically twisted. They can lean to one side or another, giving a windswept effect, but it is extremely difficult to plant semi-trained trees together as a natural looking group when they are already twisted.

A good number of trees to start with is five. This will give you a pleasing arrangement and is not too complicated. Remember that group plantings use a single variety of tree. To try and plant different varieties together is not normally effective and can look messy. Nevertheless underplantings of small grasses and moss etc. can be used to enhance the group.

To avoid spending too much, why not go to your local garden centre and look through their collection of houseplants. All varieties that grow in a tree-like manner, and have smallish leaves, are suitable for conversion into forest groups.

When deciding on the individual plants that you will need, don't forget that it will be your aim to plant a group that looks as natural as possible. You will need trees that vary in both height and trunk thickness. In natural forests you would be unlikely to see all trees the same height and age.

As far as the arrangement is concerned, you should place your trees in the approximate positions that you think would be the most effective. Try it out on a large sheet of paper, and when you have finalized the arrangement you can mark the positions on the paper so that you will remember them when it is time to pot up. The mistake to avoid when arranging your trees is the natural feeling that the small ones should be in the front, and larger ones in the back. Consider for a moment that you are looking at a group on top of a hill. You will find that the trees in front of the group look larger then those at the back. With a group of bonsai you are trying to reproduce the same perspective as that in nature: the larger trees therefore, should be planted towards the front of your group, reducing in size towards the back. Another way of enhancing your group, giving it space and distance, is to make sure that no two trees, especially in a small group like the one you are planning, are on a direct line either from front to back, or from side to side.

A sketch will help you plan your group by showing the rough positions of each tree. Nevertheless, from my own experience I have always found it easier actually to move the trees around themselves, just bearing in mind the basic design that you would like to obtain.

Having experimented with the position of each tree you will have formed the basis of the group. Now is the time to prune off some of the unwanted branches that obstruct the view or spoil the perspective. You can then start planting. If the roots do not need trimming, then you can proceed in exactly the same way for potting a group as you would for potting a single tree.

Finish any necessary pruning when you have completed the planting. If you do not want an upright group, then you can wire each individual tree to a slant just off the vertical, giving the effect of a windswept hillside. This can also be effected by initially planting the trees at an angle.

Rock plantings

Rocks are often an essential ingredient in bonsai tree cultivation and their use is widespread, even used simply as pots in which to plant a single tree. With large interestingly-shaped rocks that have a profusion of crevices, smaller trees can be planted in any natural holes to produce the effect of a mountainside. This can be enhanced with the use of dwarf underplantings near to the trees.

Rocks are widely collected, especially in the Far East. They are considered valuable items in their own right, and nearly everywhere you go in the world, you will find interestingly-shaped rocks to use with bonsai.

Although these plantings are of considerable interest, perhaps the most captivating one is where the roots of a tree are used to straddle the rock. The rock itself is placed in a bonsai pot and the roots of the tree growing over it are encouraged to grow down into the soil below. This type of rock planting is particularly suitable for tropical trees, such as *Ficus* varieties. They grow quickly, and the roots will cling onto the rock. I am sure that everyone has seen pictures of *Ficus* (Giant Banyans) growing in the jungle over ruins in just this way. With temperate trees *Acer trifidum* (trident maple) is the variety most commonly used to produce this effect as its roots behave in the same manner and, like *Ficus,* their roots will cling to whatever they are growing over. They will also grow into each other as well, sometimes giving an attractive interlacing of root growth that is fascinating.

The first thing you will need to plant a tree over a rock is a tree with roots that are long enough to go over your rock and into the soil at the base. As bonsai trees are root pruned on a regular basis, it is often better to start a new rock planting with younger material that has not had its roots pruned. If you find your selected tree does not have roots that are long enough, it will have to be grown on for at least one year to produce the roots that you will need.

In your mind's eye, you should have the basic position in which your tree will be over the rock. Make small loops of copper wire and cement them to the rock in various positions; when the tree straddles the rock the roots can then be tied into position so that they will not grow away from the rock. After the eyelets are securely stuck, tie either stout string or copper wire to each of them. Next, into the crevices of the rock where the tree is to be planted, work in a sticky wet layer of mud (50% peat/50% loam, with no added grit). Take your tree out of its growing pot and very gently tease out the roots using your fingers and a stick; washing them regularly under running water to help untangle the mess. When this has been done, divide the roots over the rock.

The tree is now sitting on its new home. You can remove some of the roots, but be careful not to prune too many unless the main roots are sufficiently thick to maintain the health of the tree. Tie the roots down, making sure you protect them with pieces of rubber or plastic. The whole plant can now be treated as a normal tree, and potted in exactly the same way as any other, using the appropriate potting compost, but making sure that the lower ends of the roots are planted securely into the compost contained in the pot.

Roots that are exposed should be smeared with a layer of wet peat and compost. This should not be too thick as the roots should be encouraged to grow into it and down towards the pot, and not at an angle away from the rock. Using plastic film, cover the whole of the rock where the roots are, leaving a small gap around the trunk of the tree so that water can be added if it starts to dry out.

Although you should top prune when needed, the newly planted rock bonsai should remain undisturbed for a year, after which time you can remove the plastic film. Over the next few months the action of watering will gradually remove the outer layer of composts that you have spread over the upper roots. The roots will slowly become revealed.

Chinese rock plantings (Saikei)

Although perhaps not bonsai in the purist sense of the word, tray landscapes consisting of rocks and small plants, are an integral part of the same philosophy. The art of bonsai is to miniaturize a variety of tree that is normally considerably larger. Bonsai is the representation of a large tree or trees on a small scale. Nevertheless the tree itself is of prime importance in every bonsai planting. On the other hand, Chinese rock landscapes reduce the scale of things even further: the rocks themselves become mountains. In this type of planting the rocks are of prime importance, and the small plants which represent trees growing in them are only of secondary importance. With this type of Lilliputian landscape, you are displaying a series of mountains or rocky islets that emerge from a tranquil sea. Indeed rocks may be sawn off flat at their base, enabling them to be stood upright in a container filled with water, to look like an island in a lake. Tiny figures, boats or pavilions may also be incorporated into this landscape. To use these figures etc. with bonsai proper is unusual and not generally approved in competitive displays. Nevertheless a bonsai school of thought is now begining to merge these two principles and a prominent rock can be added to a bonsai planting with one or two of these figures glued securely onto it.

When you are planning a landscape such as this, you must make sure that the pot you use is as unobtrusive as possible. Unlike other bonsai pots it will be very shallow and need not have drainage holes. The reason for this is that the miniature trees you plant are placed directly into the crevices of the rock which then form tiny pots. You can plant your small trees into this rock scene in exactly the same way as that used in planting a tree over a rock. As the holes or crevices are usually very small, watering can be a problem and evidence of drying out should be looked for on a daily basis. It is also a good idea to plant some sort of ground cover over the exposed surface of the compost, as this will tend to retain the moisture longer.

CHAPTER 8

Pests and diseases

As your indoor bonsai trees are normal trees and shrubs, only removed from their original environment, they are still susceptible to attacks by pests and diseases.

Provided the normal care and maintenance for trees is carried out, pests and disease should not prove a difficult problem. Certainly, if you look at your indoor trees regularly, then you will be able to detect the first sign of either. In many cases pests such as caterpillars, aphids etc. can be picked off the tree itself without the need for using chemicals.

The most common diseases that effect indoor bonsai are fungal in origin. These will almost always need chemical treatment.

Pests

Aphids

The most common insects to attack trees are aphids. These are small insects that can be various colours, including green, black, grey or orange. They suck the sap from the softer growing points of your plant.

A heavy infestation of aphids is normally seen quite easily. If it has passed the stage of simply picking them off, then you will need to use a chemical insecticide. This can either be a systemic insecticide i.e. one that mixes with the sap of the plant and attacks the insects as they suck the sap; or a contact insecticide that kills the insects by being sprayed onto them.

Ants can be a giveaway sign to the presence of aphids: you may find a large number of them crawling up your tree on their way to milk the honey dew that the aphids secrete. If an infestation is allowed to carry on too long, then this honey dew falls onto the leaves of the tree and sooty mould begins to form. After killing the aphids this mould should be wiped off the leaves with a damp cloth.

Caterpillar

Caterpillar generally appear in the spring and, even if you do not actually see them on your tree, evidence of their presence will be found in the holes and eaten-away parts of leaf. The best cure is to physically remove them with your fingertips.

Mealy bug (woolly aphid)

If your tree looks as though it has tiny pieces of cotton wool sticking to it, normally in clusters, you have a case of mealy bug. If there are only a few they can be removed with a cloth or finger and thumb; however, if the attack is more serious, they can be sprayed with Malathion. As the name implies, woolly aphid forms a protective layer of wool against the air, thus preventing insecticides from reaching it. The only other way to remove them is to paint a solution of methylated spirits onto them.

Red spider mite

Red spider mites, although very tiny, can cause serious problems for indoor bonsai. Like aphids they suck sap. They also form webs between the leaves and the stems, and in bad attacks this web can virtually cover your tree. The first sign of an attack by red spider mites is the discolouring of the leaves followed by small yellowish blotches all over them. Keeping a moist atmosphere around your trees will help to deter this pest. Nevertheless, immediately you see evidence of red spider mite, you should spray with a chemical insecticide to remove them.

Root mealy bug

Root mealy bug are not very common, but they may slow the natural growth of the tree and also discolour the leaves. Check for them by lifting the trees from the pot. If infested the roots will be covered in cotton wool. The treatment is to soak the root ball in a solution of insecticide such as Malathion.

Scale insects

The normal scale insect looks almost like a tiny tortoise with its legs and head retracted. They will be found along twigs, branches, and on leaves. Unlike other sap-sucking insects they don't mind where they are, as they are able to penetrate hard surfaces to remove the sap. A close watch should be kept out for scale insect as it is almost impossible to kill the adults with normal insecticides. I have found the best solution is to remove them physically with a cotton bud or even your fingertips, after which it is a good idea to spray the whole plant with a systemic insecticide to kill any young that you have not detected.

Thrips (leaf miners)
These tiny black insects hardly affect indoor bonsai in the home, but they sometimes attack trees that are kept outside during the summer. They make tiny tunnels through tissue of the leaves that look like irregular silvery lines. They are easily treated with insecticide.

Other insects such as earwigs, ants, etc. should be discouraged but they are not so dangerous as those mentioned above. Slugs, snails and small worms should also be removed. Occasionally ants will form a nest in the root ball of a tree and to get rid of them you should treat them with a proprietary brand of ant killer.

White fly
The first sign of these pests are tiny white moths that will fly up when the plant is disturbed. Sometimes they can occur in great numbers. Although the fly itself is the first sign of an attack, it is the larvae that actually do the damage. Larvae, which are greenish in colour, will be found on the undersides of the leaves where they suck the sap and, like aphids, produce a honey dew. As white fly has three stages in its life i.e. egg, larvae and adult fly, to eradicate them one has to spray with a recommended white fly killer at three to four day intervals for at least three to four weeks.

Fungal diseases

Damping off
This a fungus that attacks the stem bases of seedlings: the plants can no longer feed from their roots and fall over and die. To prevent this, always use sterilized compost for planting seeds. Do not overwater, and keep your seeds in an area where there is some fresh air. It is also a good idea to treat the whole of the pot that the seeds are in with Cheshunt Compound, or one that contains orthocide.

Botrytis (downy mildew)
Downy mildew can occur at any time and on any part of the plant. Particularly susceptible are soft-leafed trees. It is normally caused by too much watering and a lack of ventilation. Remove those leaves that have been infected, and treat the whole tree with a systemic fungicide.

Powdery mildew
Powdery mildew looks like a coating of fine icing sugar over the upper parts of the leaves. Like other mildew it is promoted by lack of ventilation: in other words the air around the plant remains too still. It can also be accelerated by feeding the tree excessively. Remove the infected leaves, and spray with a sulphur fungicide. Do not forget to improve the ventilation at the same time.

Although other fungal diseases do occur, they are not so common and they can normally be treated with fungicide.

Beneficial fungus

When repotting some trees you might see a white web-like fungus growing around the root ball. This mycelium is not harmful, in fact it is beneficial to the continued health of the tree on whose roots it is growing. Do not try to remove or kill it because the tree could die without this fungus. Please note that it only lives in symbiotic relationship with a few varieties of trees.

Virus

Virus attacks on plants, including bonsai, tend not to be spoken about or, if they are, then in hushed whispers. The symptoms of a viral attack can almost always be looked on as having some other cause. The unfortunate thing about virus attacks on trees and plants is that there is normally no cure. The only hope one can possibly have is to remove completely that part of the tree that is infected, hoping that it does not spread to the rest of the tree. This portion should be burned immediately. Nevertheless the worse sometimes happen that an indoor bonsai is attacked by a virus and will eventually need to be thrown away.

Chlorosis

The initial sign of this on your tree will be a lack of the normal green in the leaf, which eventually turns yellow. The reason for this is that the plant is not manufacturing enough chlorophyll. The treatment for chlorosis is to give sequestered iron. However if you select a fertilizer that contains the normal full list of constituents the risk of disease is minimal.

Treating pests and diseases

One can, on occasions, combine an insecticide with a fungicide to give an overall effect, i.e. that of killing the insect pests and also treating fungal disease. It is advisable to carry out treatment at regular intervals throughout the year, especially during the early growing season as this can be a preventative; this means that one does not have to spray too extensively when pests or disease are detected. An instance of this is that you can spray your trees with tar oil wash during the dormant season. This has the effect of killing eggs etc. of pests such as aphid and red spider mite. Tar oil wash will also kill moss, so if your tree has moss growing around the roots, this should be covered before using the spray. Whichever treatments you elect to use, it is a good idea to alternate them so that neither the insect pest, nor the fungal problem, becomes accustomed to one form of treatment. After a certain length of time pests etc. can become immune to one particular spray control.

It is advisable to use the tables below only as a guide. Chemical treatments for both pests and diseases can change almost overnight. At one particular time the chemical DDT was in widespread use throughout the world. This has now been banned from being used.

If you take the trouble to look at the various insecticides and fungicides in your local garden centre or garden shop, you will soon find those that are recommended to treat the most common problems that you are likely to experience with regard to pests and disease.

Insecticides: treatment for pests

Insecticide	Pests treated
Derris	Aphid, red spider mite, small caterpillars and thrips.
Dimethoate	Aphid, white fly, red spider mite, scale and thrips.
Fenitrothion	Caterpillars and aphid.
Malathion	Aphid, thrips, red spider mite, scale, mealy bugs and white fly.
Permethrin	White fly, aphid and caterpillars.
Pirimicarb	Aphid.
Pirimiphos-methyl	All foliar pests and caterpillars.

Fungicides: treatment for diseases

Fungicide	Diseases treated
Benomyl	Mildew, blight, black spot etc.
Carbendazim	Mildew, botrytis, black spot.
Cheshunt compound (Ammonium carbonate & copper sulphate)	Damping off.
Copper carbonate (copper)	Damping off, mildew, blight, black spot etc.
Propiconazole	Mildew, rust, black spot etc.
Thiophanate-Methyl	Mildew, black spot etc.
Thiram	Black spot and mildew.

PART 2

A–Z
Selection of Tropical
Sub=tropical and Tender Bonsai

An eight year old Ficus benjamina *approximately 30 cm (12 in) tall, planted in tufa rock.*

Acacia dealbata

SILVER WATTLE OR MIMOSA

Informal Upright

Slanting

Broom

Clump

Group

Origins/type and description

Mimosa originates in Australia, and is sub-tropical.

Mimosa is evergreen. Its foliage is well known as the mimosa used by florists, with small delicate pinnate leaves. Unfortunately it does not normally flower as a bonsai. Propagation is by seed, or by stem cuttings taken late in the summer. A rooting hormone is necessary and bottom heat will encourage rooting.

Training

Main pruning should be carried out after the flowers have finished, if you are lucky enough to get them. This occurs in late winter or early spring. Main branch pruning can be carried out at any time of the year.

Wiring is done after the flowers have finished and whilst the tree is in active growth.

General care

Watering
Water requirements for mimosa are only moderate, and although you should always keep it moist, do not soak it for long periods. During the winter cut watering down unless in a warm atmosphere. Mist occasionally, but this is not essential.

Feeding
Feeding should be carried out every three to four weeks during the growing season, using a general purpose feed preferably fairly low in nitrogen. During the winter, provided the plant is in a cool position, this can be cut out entirely.

Repotting
This is normally done every two to three years but the tree should be relatively cool before root pruning. Good drainage is essential.

Position
It needs to be kept in a bright position during winter months, and temperatures at this time should be 5°C (41°F)–11°C (52°F). During the summer, after growth has begun, then the temperature can be increased to 22°C (72°F). The ideal position now is either in a bright window with good air circulation, or in the fresh air.

Common pest
Red spider mite.

Acacia dealbata about 15 months old, 10 cm (4 in) tall.

Bouganvillea glabra

PAPER FLOWER

Informal Upright

Slanting

Semi-cascade

Group

Over Rock

Origins/type and description

This creeper originates in the southern hemisphere, mainly Brazil, and is to be regarded as sub-tropical.

Bougainvillea is semi deciduous. It will lose a number if not all of its leaves if kept too cold in the winter months. Although a creeping climber, old plants develop very thick tree-like trunks. If cultivated correctly it will 'flower' throughout the summer months. The flowers are in fact very insignificant and merely three small spikes. What one normally thinks of as flowers are the brilliantly coloured modified leaves called bracts. Branches and twigs also carry defensive thorns.

Propagation is either by seed or by stem cuttings that are taken in the summer. Rooting hormone and bottom heat of approximately 22° C (72° F) is needed for them to root.

Training

All sucker-type growth should be removed immediately it appears unless needed for another branch. During the flowering season you can prune as required, not forgetting that you might be pruning out the flowers. The best time to prune bougainvillea thoroughly is after it has finished flowering in the autumn. From autumn and into winter, pruning should be done as and when it is required.

It is advisable to wire only the young growth, as harder wood can be very brittle.

General care

Watering
During the spring and summer the compost should be kept thoroughly moist but not sodden. If indoors during this period then misting should also be carried out. After the flowering period has ended it is advisable to keep bougainvillea as dry as possible without actually damaging the plant, only resuming watering when growth appears in the spring.

Feeding
Bougainvillea should be fed at approximately ten day intervals throughout the growing period using a low nitrogenous feed. During the winter feeding should cease altogether, unless it is in heated conditions, in which case a light feed can be given at six-weekly intervals.

Repotting
As the roots of bougainvilla tend to be fine, repotting is not normally necessary for three to four years. It should then be carried out in early spring before the new season's growth commences, and sufficient sharp sand and grit should be added to the compost for good drainage and air circulation.

Position

During the winter this should be a cool light airy spot either indoors or in a conservatory. Ideal winter temperatures are 7-12° C (45-54° F). As spring approaches move the plant into a position where it can receive sunlight. At this time temperature can be increased and during the summer it can be kept indoors in a sunny warm position.

It is hard to encourage bougainvillea to flower regularly, unless these points are adhered to.

Common pests and diseases

Aphid; scale; chlorosis.

Bougainvillea glabra *60 years old and 48 cm (19 in) tall.*

Buxus harlandii

BOX

Formal Upright

Informal Upright

Slanting

Semi-cascade

Literati

Clump

Over Rock

Miniature Landscape

(Opposite) Buxus harlandii *approximately 80 years old, 36 cm (14 in) tall.*

Origins/type and description

Box originates in Europe and Asia. This particular variety mainly comes from Taiwan and should be treated as sub-tropical or tender temperate.

Box is well known throughout Europe as growing very slowly, finally becoming a large shrub or small tree. From medieval times it has been extensively used in gardens as a dwarf clipped hedge. Nevertheless this variety is tender when grown as a bonsai and should not be exposed to frost. It has thinner and slightly longer leaves than the outside box. It is evergreen and the trunk is an attractive rough yellow brown. It has masses of small white flowers in the early spring.

Propagate by taking hardened cuttings in late summer, early autumn.

Training

Heavy pruning can be done at any time of the year and general pruning can be carried out throughout the growing season. Branches will quite often need thinning out to prevent the foliage becoming too thick. If this is not done your indoor box can start looking as though it has been topiaried rather than trained as a bonsai.

Wiring can be done at any time of the year, but watch that wires do not dig into the bark: it can take a long time for scars to disappear.

General care

Watering
Water throroughly by immersing the pot. The tree should be allowed to dry out a little more than other varieties before watering again. In hot conditions it should be misted occasionally.

Feeding
Box needs feeding only once every three to four weeks during the growing season. In winter feed only if it is in active growth.

Repotting
Repotting should take place every two to three years in the spring, before the tree comes into active growth. Root pruning is normal.

Position
During the winter the tree should be put in a bright, airy position, although not in direct sunlight. It is one of the few indoor bonsai trees that will not mind a certain amount of draught. Ideal winter temperatures are between 8° C (46° F) and 20° C (68° F). During the summer and after all danger of frost has past, Box will thrive outside, but it should be given shade from very hot sunlight.

Although slow growing, Box is a very strong tree and will withstand most adverse conditions. The biggest danger is overwatering.

Common pests
Aphid; red spider mite.

Camellia

CAMELLIA

Informal Upright

Broom

Group

Origins/type and description

It originates in sub-tropical areas of the Far East. As a bonsai it should be regarded as tender temperate.

A well known shrub or small tree with beautiful flowers in the early spring. These can be single or double and can vary in colour from white to dark red. They are sometimes scented. Camellia is evergreen. For it to flower successfully growing instructions should be closely followed. Propagation is by cuttings taken in the summer. Use rooting hormone and give bottom heat of approximately 22°C (72°F).

Although you can use a number of different camellias (it is a very large family), it is suggested that the smaller flowering varieties are most suitable for training as bonsai, e.g. *C. tsaii, C. cuspidata, C. taliensis, C. maliflora, C. sasanqua,* and hybrids such as *C.* 'Cornish Snow'.

Training

Heavy pruning should be done after flowering, and general pruning carried out throughout the growing season.

Wiring can be done throughout the year except during the flowering season. However, as the branches are more brittle during the winter months. I find early summer is the best time to wire.

General care

Watering
Keep evenly moist at all times. Use softened water and mist when hot but not in direct sunlight. Reduce watering a little in the winter.

Feeding
Feed at two-weekly intervals during the summer using a liquid feed, or use organic pellets twice during the growing season. Sequestered iron should also be given three times from spring to autumn.

Repotting
Repotting is only necessary when the tree becomes potbound, about every 4–5 years. Only prune roots by about 10% and disturb the remainder as little as possible. The compost should be ericaceous, i.e. acid.

Position
During the summer camellia is happiest outside, protected from fierce afternoon sunlight. In winter it should be in a bright cool position that is free from draughts. Winter temperature should be from 4–16°C (39–61°F). It is most important that the plant is moved as little as possible from the autumn until after flowering. Buds will fall if it is moved in bud, and also if the temperature fluctuates too much.

Common pests and diseases
Aphid; red spider mite; chlorosis.

(Opposite) Camellia *approximately 35 years old, 56 cm (22 in) tall.*

Citrus

A LARGE FAMILY INCLUDING ORANGE, LEMON, LIME AND GRAPEFRUIT

Informal Upright

Slanting

Semi-cascade

Clump

Group

Origins/type and description

Citrus fruits are native to Asia, Africa and the Mediterranean. They should be treated as sub-tropical.

This is a family of evergreen shrubs and small trees. The new shoots stay a bright green until at least a year old, and some of them are armed with thorns by the leaves. As this is a large family, it is advisable for bonsai cultivation to use those that have small fruits.

Propagation is either by seed (readily available from fruit) or by cuttings taken in the spring. These will need to be treated with rooting hormone, and given bottom heat.

Training

Heavy branch pruning can be done at any time, but young growth should be pruned back while still soft. Leaf pruning is unnecessary, but larger leaves can be removed at your discretion.

You can wire at any time during the year, but new shoots should only be wired after they become slightly hard. Citrus can be brittle and the bark can damage easily, so care should be taken when wiring.

General care

Watering
Citrus should only be kept slightly moist during the winter. In the summer it must not be allowed to dry out, but watering should still be on the moderate side. It should be mist sprayed every few days.

Feeding
Feed well during the growing season, i.e. once every ten days. As the winter approaches, cut the feed down until it is almost non existent during that period. Feed with sequestered iron occasionally.

Repotting
As citrus has a fairly weak root system repot only every three to four years, in the spring. Care should be taken to do as little damage to roots as possible. After repotting keep citrus on the dry side.

Position
Place in a cool position indoors during the winter, with a temperature not less than 8°C (46°F). At the other end of the scale, temperature should not rise above 13°C (55°F) during the winter, otherwise the dormancy needed for this variety will be interrupted.

Immediately danger of frost has passed citrus should be placed outside in full sunlight for as long as possible.

Common pests and diseases
Aphid; mealy bug; scale; mildew.

(Opposite) Citrus. *This is one of many types that can be used and is 6 years old, 30 cm (12 in) tall.*

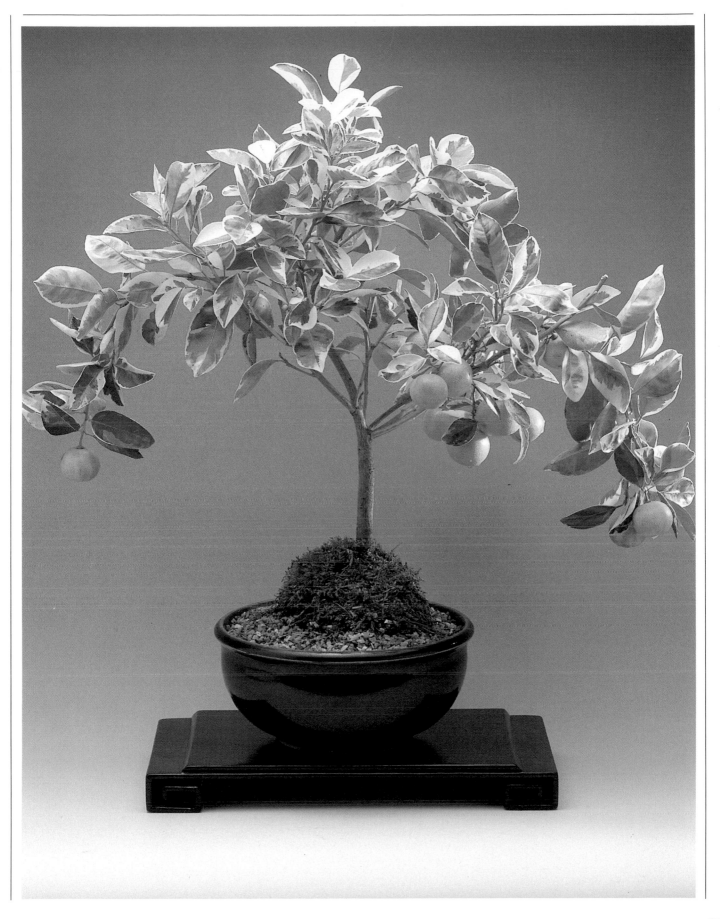

Crassula arborescens

JADE PLANT OR MONEY TREE

Informal Upright

Slanting

Over Rock

Origins/type and description

Crassula is a tree-like succulent that originates in South Africa. It should be considered sub-tropical.

It is evergreen and, although a succulent, grows in a tree-like manner and makes an interesting addition to an indoor bonsai collection. It has thick fleshy green leaves and, given the right conditions, will flower with white/pink flowers about the beginning to middle of winter.

Propagation is by cuttings that have been allowed to dry for about two weeks. Use a dry mixture to strike these cuttings and give them some bottom heat. Once they have rooted they can be potted on and watered thoroughly.

Training

Pruning may be carried out at any time of year, and you can improve its tree-like appearance by taking out some of the inside and crossing branches.

Wiring can be used, but with correct pruning should not be needed.

General care

Watering
The jade plant can survive with little water but it is advisable not to let it dry out during the summer. In the winter, especially if it is kept cool, it need not be watered for about three to four weeks at a time.

Feeding
Slow growing and therefore needs a general purpose fertilizer every four weeks during the growing season but not during the winter.

Repotting
This is best done every three to four years before growth starts in the spring. It need only be pruned back by about 10% of the root ball. Provide bottom heat afterwards to encourage re-rooting. After repotting, keep on the dry side.

Position
This tree can be kept indoors throughout the year and is resistant to changes in atmosphere. Ideal winter temperature would be between 10° C (50° F) and 18° C (64° F). It should be kept in a sunlit window as much as possible throughout the year, but a little away from the glass so that the root ball does not dry too quickly. During the summer it can go outside for a rest period.

Common pests and diseases
Scale; mealy bug; mildew.

Crassula arborescens *26 years old, 46 cm (18 in) tall.*

Cycas revoluta

SAGO PALM

Informal Upright

Origins/type and description

The family of cycas comes from different parts of the world but
C. circinnalis originates in China and is tropical.

Cycas is an extremely slow growing evergreen. It has palm-like leaves
with sharp points to them. However it is hardly related to palms. When
young the trunk is bulbous in shape but with age adopts a more tree-like
shape. In primeval times the cycas appeared after the original ferns and
they bridge the gap between ferns and true trees as we know them today.

Propagation is by removing small bulbs that grow on the outside of
the trunk. These should be placed in good quality seed compost and
given ample bottom heat to encourage rooting.

Training

Minimal pruning is required beyond the removal of dead fronts. The
confinement of this variety in a small pot will keep it on the dwarf side.

Wiring is never performed on cycas.

General care

Watering
Ample watering at all times; only slightly reducing in the winter
months. Spraying is not essential, but it is beneficial.

Feeding
Feed at monthly intervals throughout the growing period, and every six
weeks during the cooler winter.

Repotting
Cycas has thick, very fleshy but tender roots, and it should only be
repotted and root pruned when absolutely necessary. This can be from
five years onwards. Repot in the coldest part of the year but after root
pruning be sure to give bottom heat to encourage new roots.

Care must be taken when repotting as roots can be damaged easily.

Position
May be kept indoors the whole year round in a warm position.
Temperatures should not fall below 15° C (59° F), but will tolerate
considerably higher temperatures than this. Choose a reasonably bright
position, but it is advisable to keep cycas out of direct sunlight. It will
also tolerate a certain amount of shade. The cycas is slow growing,
producing no more than a few leaves each year; so beware if it is
subjected to sudden shock (changes in temperature, light levels etc.)
because it can lose all its leaves. If this happens don't throw the plant
away as, with patience, new leaves will be produced. But be patient: it
could take up to two years.

Common pests and diseases
Red spider mite; scale; damping off.

(Opposite) Cycas revoluta
*approximately 30 years
old, 25 cm (10 in) tall.*

70

Ehretia buxifolia

(syn. *Carmona microphylla*)   FUKIEN TEA

Formal Upright

Informal Upright

Slanting

Semi-cascade

Broom

Literati

Raft

Group

Miniature Landscape

Origins/type and description

This tree-like shrub originates in Southern China and other parts of South East Asia, and is tropical.

Fukien tea is evergreen with very small leaves that are dark green and shiny. The trunk is fairly smooth and a beige to brown colour. It has tiny flowers throughout the year if the conditions are warm enough, and these can be followed by small green berries which if they do not fall, will eventually turn a dark red.

Propagation is either by seed or cuttings that have been given bottom heat.

Training

Heavy branch pruning can be carried out at any time, but general pruning should wait until the new shoots have eight to ten leaves. As the leaves are very small, leaf cutting is not needed.

Wiring can be done at any time of the year during the growing season, but it is often unnecessary as pruning can be used to shape satisfactorily.

General care

Watering
Keep well watered at all times of the year, only reducing slightly during the winter months. Do not, however, allow it to stand in water. Fukien tea benefits from having its leaves sprayed occasionally.

Feeding
Feed approximately every two weeks throughout the growing season, reducing this frequency to four-weekly intervals during the winter if it is fairly cool.

Repotting
This is carried out every two to three years. After root pruning the plant should be kept slightly drier, not fertilized, and given a little more heat to encourage root growth.

Position
Fukien tea can be kept indoors the whole year round. It should be in a bright position, but receiving direct sunlight for only an hour or so a day. Ideal temperature for the winter months is 12–22°C (54–72°F). It can remain indoors throughout the year but on a hot sunny day a rest outside will help it. If it remains indoors in the summer, then the pot should be kept in the shade to avoid it becoming overheated.

Common pests and diseases
Aphid; red spider mite; scale; chlorosis.

Ehretia buxifolia *approximately 15 years old, 40 cm (16 in).*

72

Eugenia

Informal Upright

Slanting

Group

Origins/type and description

The eugenia family have widespread origins from Brazil to Australia. They should be regarded as sub-tropical.

Eugenia is evergreen and has dark green ovate leaves with a distinct drooping point at the end. They are formed in pairs and are very close together with virtually no leaf petiole (stalk). When young the new leaves have a very pleasing bronze colour. The trunk and branches are medium to dark reddish-brown and smooth. In the spring it can have pretty, small, white, cup-shaped flowers, which may be followed by dark red fruits that are edible.

Propagation is by seed.

Training

Eugenia grows very vigorously and should be pruned back hard. This pruning will also help to keep the leaves smaller than they would be normally. Leaf pruning can be done but it is impractical and direct branch pruning achieves better results.

When wiring, be very careful as branches are on the brittle side. Only wire when the plant is in active growth, but rely more on pruning to achieve the shape that you need.

General care

Watering
Keep moist throughout the year, although watering can be reduced during less active growth in the colder months. Spray with water whenever possible. As the leaves are dark green, if you are in a hard water area wipe the leaves clean every few days.

Feeding
Feed regularly throughout the growing season at two weekly intervals and about once every five weeks during the winter months.

Repotting
Usually carried out every two years or so. After repotting keep the roots warm to encourage new feeding roots to grow.

Position
During the winter months keep in a cool position, ranging from 8°–20° C (46°–68° F). Eugenia appreciates a bright position but will stand less light than some other varieties. Being sub-tropical it benefits from extended periods outdoors after all danger of frost has ceased. If the tree comes into flower before night frosts are completely finished, it helps to have it pollinated by putting it outside in a sunny spot during the day.

Common pests
Scale; mealy bug.

(Opposite) Eugenia *approximately 6 years old, 23 cm (9 in) tall.*

Ficus

JAVA WILLOW, BANYAN, FIG VARS.

Informal Upright

Slanting

Semi-cascade

Cascade

Clump

Raft

Over Rock

Origins/type and description

Apart from *Ficus carica*, most of these originate in the jungles of South East Asia. They are tropical.

Ficus is mainly evergreen and with various leaf shapes: some of them are small and shiny; others, like the well known indoor rubber plant, have much larger leaves. It is very fast growing, and you could have an old-looking tree after only a few years. An interesting point about many of the ficus family is that they grow aerial roots. These can be trained down into the soil to give an extremely aged looking appearance. They are very versatile tropical trees, and can be adapted to virtually every style. They are particularly suitable for growing over rocks as their roots will quickly intertwine.

Propagation is easy by taking cuttings, even those that are much thicker than usual. It does not require a rooting hormone, but you can always add one if you wish. To encourage rapid re-rooting, give bottom heat of at least 24°C (75°F). Ficus can also be succesfully air layered.

It is suggested that the best ficus to use for training as bonsai are those with smaller leaves like *F. benjamina, F. brevifolia, F. diversifolia, F. falcata, F. infectoria, F. pumila* var. *minima,* and *F. radicans.*

Training

Pruning can be carried out throughout the year. Remember to cut back to a bud that faces in a direction that you wish the branch to grow. When cutting they will often exude a milky sticky sap, but this soon dries up. A certain amount of leaf pruning can also be done.

Wiring can be done at any time of the year but, as the tree grows quickly, be careful to remove the wire before it digs into the bark. Young growth can also be trained on ficus simply by bending it with one's fingers. If this is done two or three times, the tree will assume the shape that you want.

General care

Watering
Ficus should be kept moist during the whole of the growing season, but when the temperature is lowered, such as in the winter, then it should be watered sparingly. Having said that, although the frequency of watering is less than during the summer months, it should still be thoroughly soaked throughout the root ball when it is watered.

Feeding
Use either a specific bonsai fertilizer or, if that is not available, then an indoor plant fertilizer, and feed at approximately two week intervals. During the winter when growth is less, it should only be fed every four to six weeks.

Repotting
Normally required every two to three years just before the new growth starts. With ficus in particular, you can repot at almost any time of the year provided you are able to give the newly root-pruned tree adequate bottom heat to encourage the formation of new roots.

Position
May be kept indoors throughout the year at temperatures preferably no lower than 15° C (59° F). It will stand lower temperatures, but it is important that conditions should not be allowed to fluctuate wildly. Ficus does not like draughts at all, but it will tolerate a lower light level than some other varieties. Brief spells outside will be beneficial during summer months.

Common pests and diseases
Scale; Anthracnose fungus.

Ficus *growing over a rock. This tree is approximately 45 years old, 71 cm (28 in) tall.*

Fuchsia

LADY'S EAR DROPS, BALLERINA TREE

Informal Upright

Slanting

Semi-cascade

Cascade

Literati

Group

Origins/type and description

It originates from South America, Central America, as well as New Zealand, and should be regarded as sub-tropical to tender temperate.

Depending on conditions, it is semi-deciduous. Some are hardy in temperate regions so it is suggested you choose as an indoor bonsai the more tender varieties with smaller, less showy, flowers for training. With proper cultivation, you can enjoy the flowers from spring to autumn.

Propagation is by cuttings taken in the spring and summer.

Training

Main branch pruning should be carried out in the spring before flowering or in the autumn after flowering as finished. Regular pruning of growing points should be carried out to encourage a bushy habit and good flowering.

Wiring can be done during the growing season. Do not water for a few days before wiring. Branches break easily, so be very careful.

General care

Watering
Keep moist during spring to autumn, and water by plunging. Provided it is cool in the winter, watering should be reduced to the minimum needed. Mist frequently during the growing season, less in the winter.

Feeding
Feed at two weekly intervals throughout the growing season. Alternate a general feed with one low in nitrogen. During the winter only feed every six weeks with a weaker solution.

Repotting
Repot yearly in the early spring using a good quality bonsai or general purpose compost.

Position
It is essential that this variety is kept cool during the winter: 4–9° C (39–48° F) is ideal. Even in the winter fuchsia must be kept relatively humid, so it will not be happy in a centrally-heated room. It should be in a bright position with little or no sun. In the summer, it will flourish outside but may be kept indoors in a bright position.

Common pests and diseases
Red spider mite; white fly; black spot.

Fuchsia *approximately 8 years old, 30 cm (12 in) tall.*

Gardenia jasminoides

GARDENIA

Informal Upright

Slanting

Semi-cascade

Cascade

Clump

Origins/type and description

This tree originates in South East Asia and it is regarded as tropical.

Gardenia is evergreen. It has shiny green leaves, and flowers profusely in the spring with either a single six-pointed flower or a double flower. These flowers are highly scented and almost overpowering for some in their sweetness.

Propagation is by cuttings taken in the spring. Rooting hormone is used and a bottom heat of about 27° C (80° F).

Training

Heavy branches can be pruned at any time; younger branches should be pruned back hard after the flowers have finished. New growth is pruned back to two or three leaves as it grows.

Wiring can be done at any time, but is best near the beginning of the growing season, and after the flowers are over.

General care

Watering
Gardenia should be kept moist at all times although it requires less water in the winter. It is a good idea to use soft rainwater with this variety.

Feeding
Fertilizer should be given in liquid form approximately once every ten days during the growing season, but not whilst the plant is in flower. The fertilizer should be fairly high in nitrogen. Gardenias will also benefit from one or two applications of sequestered iron during the spring and summer.

Repotting
As this variety needs to have good air circulation around the roots, the root ball should be checked yearly in the spring. If at all stale or stagnant, the compost should be changed, incorporating a layer of gravel or grit at the base of the pot. The compost should have sharp sand and grit mixed in with it.

Position
This tree can be kept indoors the whole year round near a bright window that faces north to north-east. To ensure good flowering, the temperature in the winter should not drop below 15° C (59° F). Maximum temperature during this period would be in the range of 24° C (75° F). To stop flower buds dropping, it is advisable to keep the temperature as even as possible and to avoid all draughts. During the summer brief periods outside are beneficial, but not essential.

Common pests and diseases
Caterpillar; aphid; thrip (flower buds); chlorosis.

(Opposite) Gardenia jasminoides *5 years old, 20 cm (8 in) tall.*

Hibiscus rosa=sinensis

ROSE OF CHINA, ROSE MALLOW

Informal Upright

Slanting

Semi-cascade

Group

Origins/type and description

Originating in China and the islands of the Pacific, it should be regarded as tropical.

Although the dark green leaves are somewhat large for a bonsai, it is grown for its large papery flowers which can range in colour from white to deep red. These do not last long but as it flowers throughout the growing season you will always have colour. It is evergreen unless the temperature drops too low.

Propagation is by cuttings taken with a heel from late spring to early summer. Rooting hormone and bottom heat help the cuttings to root.

Training

Main branch pruning should be done after flowering but general pruning can be carried out at any time. Hibiscus flowers on new wood.

Wiring is possible at any time the tree is in active growth. Allow new growth to harden off a little before wiring.

General care

Watering
It should be kept moist at all times, and only allowed to become slightly drier in the winter. Watering is best by immersion. Dry conditions can cause leaf and bud loss. Misting should be done throughout the growing period.

Feeding
Feeding should be done at ten day intervals throughout the flowering season. This is reduced to once a month in the winter.

Repotting
Hibiscus should be repotted every other year. Roots should be lightly pruned by about 20%.

Position
To keep indoors the whole year, choose a warm bright position that is shaded from afternoon sunlight. Winter temperature should be from 15–22° C (59–72° F). The higher the temperature, the more water it will need. In the summer hibiscus benefits from brief spells outside, although it can also stay indoors and be placed by an open window.

Common pests
Red spider mite; aphid.

Hibiscus rosa-sinensis *approximately 10 years old, 60 cm (24 in) tall.*

Jacaranda ovalifolia

(syn. *J. mimosifolia*)   JACARANDA

Informal Upright

Slanting

Clump

Group

Miniature Landscape

Origins/type and description

This tree originates in South America and is tropical.

Jacaranda is semi-deciduous. In its wild form it has the most beautiful racemes of mauve to purple flowers, but these are unusual as a bonsai. Its main interest is the very delicate fern-like leaves it produces. With bonsai treatment these leaves will be considerably reduced in size.

Training

Branch pruning can be done at any time, and pruning of the new growth should be carried out as and when necessary.

Wiring can be done at any time the tree is in active growth, but it is better to wait until the new shoots have become slightly hardened.

General care

Watering
Jacaranda likes a moderate amount of water throughout the growing season and during the winter it should be kept on the dry side. It benefits from being mist sprayed frequently, especially during hot dry weather.

Feeding
Feed every two to three weeks during the summer and about every five weeks during the winter if kept in warm conditions; otherwise feeding can be stopped during this time.

Repotting
This is normally necessary after two to three years and should be carried out in the spring before the new growth commences.

Position
During the winter this tree should be kept in a bright sunlit window. The ideal winter temperature is 15°C (50°F) up to 24°C (75°F). If kept indoors during the summer, jacaranda should be moved away from very hot sunshine, and placed where it has a certain amount of shade. It will, however, be quite happy outside during the summer months, if given a certain amount of shade.

Common pests
Aphid; scale.

Jacaranda ovalifolia seedling group just over 1 year old, 20 cm (8 in) tall.

Juniperus californica

CALIFORNIAN JUNIPER

Formal Upright

Informal Upright

Slanting

Semi-cascade

Cascade

Literati

Clump

Raft

Group

Over Rock

Origins/type and description

This tree originates in South West United States of America and is sub-tropical.

This juniper is evergreen. It has a typical segmented leaf structure together with a brown bark that flakes easily. This gives a rugged aged look to even quite a young tree.

Propagation is by seed.

Training

Pruning can be carried out on heavy branches throughout the year. On new green growth pruning should be done by pulling out the segments of the leaf. If these are cut they will turn brown and the ends will wither. Only hardened growth should ever be cut on this juniper.

Wiring can be carried out at any time of the year.

General care

Watering
Keep moist throughout the year but not saturated. During the winter, if kept indoors, it will require less water than in the summer. Juniper benefits from being sprayed over occasionally.

Feeding
Feed at between two and three week intervals throughout the growing season. If kept cool in the winter then feeding should cease, but a little should be given if it is warm.

Repotting
This can be done at three to four yearly intervals. Good drainage should be incorporated in the compost and after the initial watering the tree should be kept on the dry side for about three weeks.

Position
A bright position indoors but not near a window is ideal during the winter. Temperature should be between 7° C (45° F) and 13° C (55° F). During the summer this tree can still be kept indoors but will benefit from one or two weeks outside in the sun.

Common pest
Red spider mite.

Juniperus californica *approximately 18 years old, 46 cm (18 in) tall.*

86

Lagerstroemia indica

CHINESE CRAPE MYRTLE

Informal Upright

Slanting

Raft

Origins/type and description

This tree-like shrub originates in China and should be regarded as sub-tropical.

It is deciduous and has mauve to lilac flowers, sometimes white or pink, in late summer. It also has a very attractive coloured trunk, with the main branches being mottled pink, cinnamon and grey. The outer bark tends to shed occasionally.

Propagation is by seed. Cuttings can also be taken in the late summer and given rooting hormone and bottom heat.

Training

If you wish the tree to flower, then main pruning should be done either in the late autumn after flowering, or early spring before the leaves appear. Flowers are borne in groups at the end of a season's growth and, therefore, if you cut this growth off you will not get any flowers.

Wiring should be done during the early to middle part of the summer when the plant is in full growth. Be careful not to damage the branches.

General care

Watering
Keep evenly moist during the summer months, gradually accustoming the tree to be slightly drier before it flowers. Recommence good watering after flowering and pruning, but during the winter this should again be reduced, especially if being kept in a cool atmosphere. This shrub also appreciates being sprayed during the summer months.

Feeding
Feed approximately every two weeks until a month before flowering. A general purpose fertilizer should be alternated with a tomato fertilizer that is low in nitrogen. During the winter no feeding is needed.

Repotting
If using a very small pot, you may need to repot every year; otherwise every two to three years will normally be adequate. This should be done before the buds open in the spring.

Position
During the winter place in a bright airy position, close to a window but protected from very strong sunlight. This tree prefers to be kept cool during this period and a temperature of 7–12° C (45–54° F) is ideal. Higher temperatures will produce growth too early; Chinese crape myrtle needs a dormant season. During the summer it can be placed outside after all danger of frost has passed. Alternatively it can remain indoors near an open window.

Common pests and diseases
Aphid; mildew.

(Opposite) Lagerstroemia indica *approximately 20 years old, 51 cm (20 in) tall.*

Murraya paniculata

JASMINE ORANGE

Informal Upright

Slanting

Semi-cascade

Clump

Raft

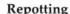

Group

Origins/type and description

This tree originates in India and is tropical.

An evergreen with smooth light brown bark. Its leaves are pinnate and bright green. Jasmine flowers unevenly but any time of the year, and the white flowers have a strong sweet smell. Berries that turn red and look like elongated miniature oranges follow the flowers.

Propagation is by planting the complete red fruits just as or before they fall. If cuttings are used they should be taken as the new wood is beginning to go hard, but bottom heat of 30° C (85° F) will be needed.

Training

Pruning can be carried out at any time of the year but watch for flower buds, as these occur on new growth.

Wiring can also be done any time of the year, but it is best carried out when the tree is in active growth.

General care

Watering
Jasmine should never be allowed to dry out. Immersion is probably the best way of watering.

Feeding
A general feed applied once every ten days to two weeks throughout the growing season is needed. This can be discontinued if cool in the winter, but if kept warm, then feeding should carry on approximately once every three to five weeks.

Repotting
An easy tree to repot. It should be done every two to three years and given bottom heat to encourage rooting after this has been completed.

Position
Apart from during very warm summer weather, this tree can be kept indoors in a bright position throughout the year. It needs plenty of light, but if exposed to very bright sunshine the pot and root ball should be kept shaded. During the winter fairly high temperatures of 13° C (55° F) are required.

Common pests and diseases
White fly; aphid; red spider mite; mildew.

Murraya paniculata approximately 60 years old, 56 cm (22 in) tall.

Myrtus

MYRTLE

Formal Upright

Informal Upright

Slanting

Semi-cascade

Broom

Clump

Raft

Group

Origins/type and description

Myrtles are a widespread family that originate in such places as Southern Europe, South America, Africa and Tropical Asia. The variety normally grown as a bonsai tree is regarded as being tender temperate.

Myrtle is evergreen and has small, shiny, dark green leaves. During the summer it flowers profusely: the white petals surround a prominent group of fine golden stamens. After the flowers are over they are followed by red to blackberry-coloured berries.

Propagation is by sowing the seed, but these take a considerable length of time to germinate. Another method is to take stem cuttings in mid-summer and treat them with a rooting hormone.

Training

Main pruning of heavy branches can be carried out at any time of the year. Myrtle is a very vigorous grower, so during the early spring it should be pruned back regularly. Inner small branches should also be thinned out to stop the tree looking as though it has been topiaried. Pruning should cease from late spring or early summer to allow the tree to flower.

Wiring can be carried out at any time whilst the tree is in active growth, but after the initial training has been completed pruning will usually be adequate.

General care

Watering
Water with soft water and keep moist throughout the growing season. Myrtle should not be allowed to stand in water as the roots will rot. During the winter watering should be cut down considerably, provided the myrtle is in a cool position. During the summer spray mist the leaves as frequently as possible. In the winter it appreciates being sprayed two or three times a week.

Feeding
During the growing season myrtle should be fed at fortnightly intervals using a general purpose fertilizer. In the winter, provided the tree is dormant, feeding can cease until the tree starts growing again in the early spring.

Repotting
Repotting is carried out every two to three years, before the new spring growth commences.

Position
In the winter keep in a very cool but bright position. It likes some sunlight during the winter. Ideal temperature is 5–11° C (41–52° F). It can stand higher temperatures but prefers to have a dormant period so

the lower end of the temperature scale is preferable. During the summer it benefits from being kept outside in the fresh air. It should be allowed some sunshine but protected from the very hot afternoon sun.

Myrtus over 100 years old, 46 cm (18 in) tall.

Common pests
Aphid; red spider mite.

Nandina domestica

SACRED BAMBOO

Informal Upright

Clump

Group

Origins/type and description

This variety originates in India, China and Japan. Although hardy against light frost, when trained as a bonsai it should be treated as sub-tropical.

Generally speaking nandina is an evergreen but in very cold weather it will shed its leaves. The leaves are long, elegant, and pinnate. Their colouring can range from light to dark green, or even light red to dark red, and mauve, varying from season to season, and plant to plant. Nandina is reluctant to branch from its trunk, and normally it is planted as a multi-trunk group. It will occasionally flower in masses of small, white to yellow flowers in mid to late summer. If pollinated these can be followed by attractive red berries.

Propagation is by seed that must be stratified first.

Training

Pruning can be carried out at any time of the year. Nandina is cut back hard to encourage it to branch. It doesn't matter where you cut as there are many dormant buds invisible to the naked eye. Leaf pruning can also be done in the growing season or the leaves can merely be shortened if they become overly large.

General care

Watering
Keep moist at all times during the winter. Watering can be reduced as the tree will be semi-dormant if kept in a cool position. In the summer it can be sprayed with water every few days.

Feeding
Feed regularly at two weekly intervals using a low nitrogen feed throughout the summer. In the winter this can be reduced to four weekly intervals.

Repotting
Repotting becomes necessary after three to four years.

Position
During the winter this tree should be kept cool at a temperature of between 7° C (45° F) and 15° C (60° F). It can withstand higher temperatures, but will require more water. Nandina should be placed in a bright position, and does not mind a certain amount of sunlight. In the summer it is best placed outside in the fresh air but shaded from hot afternoon sunlight.

Common pests
Aphid; red spider mite.

Nandina domestica approximately 15 years old, 46 cm (18 in) tall.

Olea europaea

OLIVE

Formal Upright

Informal Upright

Slanting

Semi-cascade

Clump

Group

(Opposite) *Olea europaea*
6 years old, 25 cm (6 in)
tall.

Origins/type and description

This tree originates in the Mediterranean area. Some of these trees are very ancient, indeed going back thousands of years. It is regarded as sub-tropical.

Olive is an evergreen. Some varieties have long thin leaves, others have smaller and rounder leaves. The upper side of the leaf is shiny dark green, the underside has almost a greyish fur on it. In its wild state it flowers and fruits profusely, giving the ubiquitous olive oil. As a bonsai, it is rare to flower. If it does, the flowers are small greenish white and fragrant. The bark of the olive is a greyish colour, and when the olive becomes old the trunk can take on incredible shapes.

Propagation is by taking cuttings with a heel or by seed.

Training

Pruning can be done at any time of the year but it is advisable to prune back immediately you think a branch is becoming too long. Allow new shoots to develop no more than two or three pairs of leaves before pruning. Leaf cutting is unnecessary.

Wiring can be done at any time of the year, but it is advisable during the growing season.

General care

Watering
The olive should be kept a little dryer than other trees. Nevertheless, when you do water, water thoroughly. During winter months it can be allowed to dry out even more than in the summer. However, the humidity around the tree should still be maintained at a fairly high level by misting.

Feeding
A light liquid feed should be given at two week intervals throughout the growing season. It should not be fed at all during the winter.

Repotting
This is normally needed every two to three years but it can be longer. When repotting incorporate about 35% sharp sand into the mixture.

Position
This tree can be kept indoors throughout the winter in a bright position and will stand sunlight through a window for a few hours a day. Winter temperatures should be approximately 8–18° C (46–64° F); night time temperatures should be lower but not down below 5° C (41° F). After danger of frost has passed, you can put this tree outside where it will benefit from the fresh air.

Common pest
Scale.

Pinus halepensis

ALEPPO PINE

Formal Upright

Informal Upright

Slanting

Semi-cascade

Literati

Group

Over Rock

(Opposite) Pinus
halepensis *5 years old,
20 cm (8 in) tall.*

Origins/type and description

This tree is widely seen in the Mediterranean area and also in western Asia. It is regarded as sub-tropical.

The Aleppo pine is evergreen. It is unusual as a pine tree in as much that when it is trained as a bonsai it is pruned in a similar way to junipers. In the wild the needles can be up to 10 cm long, whereas, trained as a bonsai, they are no more than 2 cm. The trunk is a lightish brown colour and the bark is characteristically pine-like. It does not flower.

Propagation is by seed which germinate readily.

Training

Unlike other pines, it does not develop candles in the spring when trained as a bonsai. If you look carefully you will see tiny buds in the axils of the needles at irregular intervals along new growth. Pruning is done by either carefully cutting above one of these buds, or by pinching out. Do this regularly, to stop the tree developing long needles.

Wiring can be done any time of the year.

General care

Watering
Watering should only be done when the tree has almost dried out. It is very adaptable to changes in watering, but only if these changes take place over longish periods of time. Sudden changes in frequency of watering may damage or even kill it.

Feeding
Feed at regular two weekly intervals throughout the growing season. This should be reduced during the winter months unless the tree is being kept very warm.

Repotting
Every two to three years. This variety can develop thick roots quickly, and an inspection at yearly intervals during the period when growth is at its slowest is advisable.

After repotting, new roots can be encouraged by giving the tree some bottom heat.

Position
This tree can be kept indoors throughout the winter with temperatures not lower than 5° C (41° F). This is a minimum and it is happier between 10° C (50° F) and 20° C (68° F). It should be kept in a bright position, but not in any draught at all and it benefits from being put outside when the summer is warm.

Pistacia terebinthus

PISTACHIO, CHIAN TURPENTINE TREE

Informal Upright

Slanting

Semi-cascade

Clump

Raft

Group

Origins/type and description

This tree originates in certain parts of Asia and in the Mediterranean region. It is sub-tropical.

Pistachio is an evergreen. It has small pinnate leaves that are dark green and glossy. Older trees may occasionally flower, but the flower is green and insignificant. If your tree does flower and is pollinated, then it can have small reddish fruit in the autumn.

Watch for mealy bug (Woolly aphid).

Propagation is by seed.

Training

Pruning can be done at any time of the year, cutting back to one or two leaves. Watch for growth suddenly emerging lower down on this tree. If this occurs it should be removed immediately unless you need it for another branch. Leaf cutting is not normally carried out but larger leaves or even half of the pinnate leaves can be removed.

Wiring should be done about six weeks to two months after the growing season has commenced.

General care

Watering
Although very strong and, in its native habitat, used to moderately dry conditions, this variety should be kept moist at all times. It should also be sprayed daily with tepid water, especially in hot conditions.

Feeding
Feeding should be every two weeks using a bonsai or general purpose fertilizer during the growing season. If kept cool in the winter feeding can be done once every six weeks.

Repotting
This is normally needed after three years or when the tree has become potbound. Normal bonsai compost with some added sharp sand and grit is recommended as it does not like to stand in water.

Position
As this variety is sub-tropical it should be kept indoors whilst there is any danger of frost. The temperature should not fall below 10° C (50° F), but it will survive in lower temperatures down to about 5° C (41° F). Whilst indoors it should be in a bright position that is not too hot. After the danger of frost has passed it will benefit from being outside for a period of time.

Common pests and diseases
Scale; mealy bug; wilt; root rot.

Pistacia terebinthus. *This mountain scene is only 5 years old. The trees are 15 cm (6 in) tall.*

Podocarpus macrophyllus

KUSAMAKI, BUDDHIST PINE OR CHINESE YEW

Formal Upright

Informal Upright

Slanting

Semi-cascade

Cascade

Literati

Group

Over Rock

(Opposite) Podocarpus macrophyllus *approximately 55 years old, 90 cm (36 in) tall.*

Origins/type and description

This tree originates in the Far East; China and Japan. When growing in the wild, it is hardy. Grown as a bonsai it should be regarded as sub-tropical.

Podocarpus is a coniferous evergreen. It has similar leaf formation and shape to that of *Taxus* (yew) although the leaves are larger. The trunk is generally a slightly mottled brown. It is slow growing, and could be trained in the formal upright style, if one wished.

Propagation can be by seed but these are difficult to obtain. Otherwise take cuttings during the growing season when they have become fairly hard. Use a rooting hormone and give bottom heat to encourage formation of roots.

Training

Pruning can be carried out at any time of the year. Although a lot of needle-type evergreens are pruned by pinching out, it will be found that this variety is too hard for that. It should be pruned with sharp scissors, being careful not to cut across the leaves.

Wiring can also be done at any time, but it is advisable to wire new shoots as and when they grow to a manageable size.

General care

Watering
Keep evenly moist, and during the summer months it appreciates being sprayed every other day.

Feeding
Feed two weeks during the growing season and every six weeks in the winter, unless it is in a warm position where it will grow more freely.

Repotting
Podocarpus is slow growing and therefore will only need repotting every three to four years. Unlike other bonsai trees one should be particularly careful when pruning the roots and only lightly prune them by approximately 10–15%, as against one-third for most trees.

Position
In the winter, whilst this tree is being displayed indoors, it should be in a position where it gets little or no direct sunlight, although it should still be in a bright spot. It prefers to be cool during the winter with a minimum temperature of 5°C (41°F). Once all danger of frost has passed (though it will survive light frosts) then it can be put outside where it will be happier during the summer and early autumn. In the summer it does not need to be shaded.

Common pests and diseases
Aphid; red spider mite; mealy bug; scale.

Polyscias fruticosa

MING ARALIA

Informal Upright

Clump

Raft

Group

Over Rock

Origins/type and description

Ming aralia is found from India to the South Pacific. It is tropical.

It is evergreen and although the leaves are pinnate the leaflets are so deeply cut and irregular it is difficult to notice this. The trunk is normally light beige/brown and rough. It is well known as a houseplant but can make an interesting indoor bonsai group planting. It branches well and almost bonsai's itself, as it grows slowly and neatly.

Propagation is by cuttings taken in the spring. Use a rooting hormone and give bottom heat to a temperature of 34° C (75° F).

Training

Pruning can be carried out at any time of the year. Remove inner branches to give a more tree-like appearance. It can be leaf pruned.

With correct pruning, wiring is normally not necessary but can be carried out during the growing season.

General care

Watering
Keep moist at all times but allow to drain freely after watering. Mist over the leaves at least once a day.

Feeding
Feed at two weekly intervals during the season. Reduce this to every five or six weeks during the winter.

Repotting
Repot every two to three years in the spring. Reduce the temperature to about 10° C (50° F) for about three weeks before root pruning. Incorporate plenty of sharp sand and grit in the new compost to promote good drainage. After repotting heat should return to a minimum of 15° C (59° F).

Position
It can be kept indoors the whole year and will adapt to light conditions varying from semi shade to bright sunlight, but make any adjustment gradually. Winter temperatures should be between 15° C (59° F) and 27° C (80° F). Shade the pot during the summer months if kept indoors in hot sunlight. It likes brief periods outside in the summer sunshine, but only when the weather is hot.

Common pests and diseases
Red spider mite; scale; alternaroise fungus.

Polyscias fruticosa 5 years old, 23 cm (9 in) tall.

Punica granatum

(syn. *Nana*) POMEGRANATE

Informal Upright

Slanting

Group

Origins/type and description

This tree-like shrub originates in the Mediterranean and areas such as India, and Southern China. It is regarded as sub-tropical.

Pomegranate is semi deciduous. If kept cool in winter it loses all its leaves, and they grow again during the spring. If it is warm during the winter it will briefly lose all its leaves in the late autumn or early part of the winter. After a few weeks, these will grow again. It will then flower in late spring and early summer, producing either red or white flowers. Leaves are medium green, thin and shiny. Propagation is by taking cuttings which will need rooting hormone and bottom heat, or by seed.

Training

Pruning can be carried out at any time but if you want the tree to flower it should be allowed to elongate longer than normal. Flowers generally appear at the end of this growth. After flowering the tree should be pruned back quite severely in order for flowering to be repeated at a later date. Wiring can be done at any time but preferably not during the flowering season.

General care

Watering
Pomegranates require ample water during the summer but only a little in the winter, especially if in a cool position. The tree can be mist sprayed regularly throughout the summer months.

Feeding
Feed with a general purpose fertilizer every three weeks during the summer and alternate with a fertilizer that is low in nitrogen. If it is kept warm in the winter it will also need a little fertilizer approximately once every five or six weeks.

Repotting
Repotting and root pruning should be done every two to three years. The ideal time for this is when the tree has dropped its leaves and before the new ones break.

Position
This tree can be kept indoors throughout the year in a bright position. The ideal cool temperature would be not less than 7° C (45° F). It will, however, be happy up to 20° C (68° F), but if kept too warm the growth can be long and thin. From spring to summer it should be placed where it receives as much sunlight as possible, although it should not be right next to a window unless the pot itself is shaded. Immediately the frosts are over, it can be put outside in the sunniest spot you can find.

Common pests and diseases
Aphid; white fly; red spider mite; mildew; chlorosis.

(Opposite) Punica granatum *approximately 35 years old, 50 cm (20 in) tall.*

Pyracantha

FIRETHORN

Informal Upright

Slanting

Semi-cascade

Cascade

Broom

Raft

Group

Over Rock

Origins/type and description

Most originate in China but others come from tropical regions such as the Philippines. Can be tender temperate to sub-tropical to tropical.

Evergreen, and as its name implies, it normally bears thorns, which are fiercer on temperate varieties. Leaves are dark green, long and shiny. White spring flowers are followed by berries in different shades of orange/red. Leaves and flowers on tropical firethorns are usually smaller than those on temperate trees.

Propagation is by cuttings taken in the autumn or by seed.

Training

Branch and general pruning can be carried out at any time. Remove any unwanted new growth from the trunk.

Wiring should be done during the growing season and removed at the end of the growing season.

Be careful of the thorns as some people react badly to their prick.

General care

Watering
Keep moist at all times but a little drier in the winter. Extra water should be given when fruit is setting. Mist the leaves frequently in warm conditions.

Feeding
Feed at two weekly intervals during the growing season, reducing in the autumn. Only feed in the winter if in active growth.

Repotting
Repot every two to three years before active growth commences, and incorporate plenty of sharp sand and grit to ensure good drainage.

Position
All pyracanthas will enjoy being outside in the sunshine during the summer months. In the winter tender temperate species should be kept in a bright cool position at temperatures of between 5° C (41° F) and 12–22° C (54/72° F) Always protect pyracanthas grown as bonsai against severe frost. Temperate varieties do not mind a slight draught but others should be kept as sheltered as possible. Pyracanthas appreciate sunshine for one or two hours a day.

Common pests and diseases
Aphid; mealy bug; scale; fireblight.

Pyracantha *from the Philippines. This is planted on a rock; it is about 18 years old, 40 cm (16 in) tall.*

Rhapis humilis excelsa

HEMP PALM, LITTLE LADY PALM

Informal Upright

Group

Origins/type and description

This palm originates in the Far East, and is considered tropical.

Although a palm and not a tree, this could make an interesting addition to your collection. It has typical palm-like leaves and grows on a single stem. As the palm grows, a dark, matt brown, woven cloth forms around the trunk.

Propagation is by seed.

Training

Occasional pruning is all that is necessary. It will not branch at all and when it has reached a height that is higher than you wish, it should be pruned back to a frond.

Wiring is not needed.

General care

Watering
Keep moist at all times but not saturated. In the winter, if kept cool, watering can be reduced. Hemp palms should never be stood in water, but will appreciate a light misting every few days.

Feeding
A general fertilizer can be given throughout the growing season at three weekly intervals. This should be reduced to five or six weekly intervals in the winter months.

Repotting
It is advisable to repot as little as possible as palms do not like their roots disturbed. Nevertheless, when it becomes necessary, repot in early spring, and be sure to give as open a compost as possible using ample drainage; excess water can then drain quickly from the root ball. After root pruning give bottom heat to encourage fresh roots to develop.

Position
Choose a position not too near a sunlit window but still reasonably bright. During the winter the temperature should not be allowed to drop below 10° C (50° F) but it will be happier at a slightly higher temperature. Keep out of draughts. Rhapis can remain in the house the whole year without harm, but it will still appreciate periods outside during the summer in the fresh air.

Rattan should be treated in exactly the same way.

Common pests and diseases
Red spider mite; scale; yellow spot fungus.

Rhapis humilis excelsa *approximately 8 years old, 30 cm (12 in) tall.*

Sageretia theezans

SAGERETIA

Formal Upright

Informal Upright

Slanting

Semi-cascade

Cascade

Broom

Clump

Raft

Group

Over Rock

Origins/type and description

This tree originates in Southern China, and is tropical.

Sageretia is evergreen. It has small, shiny green leaves that are sometimes an attractive pinkish-brown when young. The trunk is a deep rich brown, and the outer bark is shed at regular intervals, giving older trees a mottled effect like that of plane trees and trident maples. Sometimes small flowers will develop if the tree is left unpruned.

Propagation is by cuttings. Rooting is encouraged by using rooting hormone and giving moderate bottom heat.

Training

Pruning can be carried out throughout the year, cutting back excess growth to one or two pairs of leaves. As this tree has very small leaves, leaf pruning is unnecessary except with oversized leaves.

Wiring is also done at any time, apart from cold periods. Be particularly careful with new growth as it is brittle when young.

General care

Watering
This tree must be kept moist at all times; in the summer it might need watering at least once a day. In hot, dry conditions, i.e. centrally-heated houses, it should be sprayed daily with tepid water.

Feeding
Feed every two weeks using a bonsai or general purpose fertilizer during the growing season. If it is warm during the winter then it will also benefit from the occasional feed.

Repotting
This is normally necessary after two to three years, when the tree is almost potbound. Before repotting allow the tree to be a little cooler than normal. Prune the roots and use a good quality open compost.

Position
This tree can be kept indoors for the whole year in a temperature not lower than 10° C (50° F). It should be situated in a bright position, but not in direct sunlight for more than about an hour a day. In the summer it will benefit from being outside, but it must be given shade from hot summer afternoon sunlight.

Common pests and diseases
Aphid; white fly; red spider mite; chlorosis.

Sageretia theezans *approximately 90 years old, 60 cm (24 in) tall.*

Schefflera brassaia actinophylla

UMBRELLA TREE

Informal Upright

Clump

Group

Over Rock

Origins/type and description

This tree originates in Australia and is tropical.

The umbrella tree is evergreen. It has fairly large leaves for a bonsai which will become smaller over the years. It has been well known for many years as an ordinary houseplant. As a bonsai it is normally planted in lava rock that has many holes so the roots can penetrate it; or as a 'Mangrove' like group. In this case aerial roots form and go down into the soil of the pot. It flowers in the wild but not as a bonsai. Unless cut back it will grow a straight trunk.

This tree is not easy to propagate but stem cuttings can be taken during the summer months. Rooting hormone and bottom heat of approximately 24° C (75° F) is needed. Seed, if obtainable, can also be used.

Training

Pruning is only necessary when this slow growing plant gets too tall. When it is pruned, it can be cut back as far as you like and will send out new leaves in a few weeks.

Wiring is difficult with this subject and should only be attempted if absolutely necessary.

General care

Watering
The trunks conserve a certain amount of water so watering is only necessary when the plant is on the dry side. Too much water can result in root rot. When watering it is necessary to saturate the plant and then let it drain thoroughly. It likes to be sprayed frequently with tepid water.

Feeding
Feed should be given once a month during the growing season and reduced during the winter months.

Repotting
If growing in a pot then repotting should be carried out evey two to three years. After a period of time trees growing over rocks should also be placed in a pot to allow the roots to travel into the compost.

Position
This tree can remain indoors the whole year round in as bright a position as possible. High light intensity will help to keep the leaves small. During the winter months the temperature should not fall below 13° C (55° F) and the tree will be happy up to 24° C (75° F).

Common pests and diseases
Red spider mite; aphid; scale; mealy bug; alternaroise fungus.

Schefflera brassaia actinophylla *6 years old, 20 cm (8 in) tall.*

Serissa foetida

TREE OF A THOUSAND STARS

Informal Upright

Slanting

Semi-cascade

Clump

Raft

Group

Over Rock

(Opposite) Serissa foetida
approximately 18 years
old, 30 cm (12 in) tall.

Origins/type and description

This tree originates in China and South East Asia. It is regarded as being sub-tropical.

Serissa is an evergreen, although with low temperatures it can drop its leaves. These can also be shed when the plant experiences sudden changes in atmospheric conditions. They should, however, quickly return. Although basically a shrub, it can make a charming indoor bonsai. As its name implies, it can be covered in small white flowers, and these normally occur from late spring to summer, although it is not unusual for serissa to flower at other times as well. The leaves are tiny and pale to dark green. Very interestingly-gnarled roots soon develop, giving the tree an aged appearance. This is a favourite subject for bonsai with both the Chinese and the Japanese.

Propagation is easily achieved by taking cuttings which root readily.

Training

Pruning can be done at any time during the year and might need to be quite severe to maintain the shape of the tree. Remove dead flowers after they have withered to encourage further flowering.

Wiring can be done at any time, although it is best during the growing season.

General care

Watering
This tree is thirsty and therefore can be stood in a tray of water in the summer months. During the winter it should still be kept reasonably moist. Spraying the leaves will also help.

Feeding
Feed at fortnightly intervals throughout the summer, decreasing to once a month during the winter.

Repotting
As this variety is normally grown in a small pot, then root-pruning and repotting should be done at two yearly intervals, before the new growth appears in the spring. When root-pruning, be prepared for the unpleasant smell the roots give off when being cut.

Position
During the winter this tree should be kept in a bright position indoors but not too hot. Ideal temperature is between 10° C (50° F) and 20° C (68° F). This tree likes sunshine, but remember if it is near glass to shade the pot and root ball to prevent them getting too hot. In the summer the tree can either be kept inside or out.

Common pests and diseases
Red spider mite; aphid; scale; mildew.

Sterculia

QUEENSLAND BOTTLE TREE OR KURRAJONG

Informal Upright

Group

Origins/type and description

This tree originates in the deserts of Australia. It can be regarded as sub-tropical to tropical.

The bottle tree is evergreen. It has largish leaves of various shapes from three pointed and elongated, to rounder and more compact. This tree has an extraordinary root structure that occurs from the way in which it has been grown.

It does not flower, and its chief attraction in being treated as an indoor bonsai is that it is incredibly resistant to bad management.

Training

Pruning can be carried out at any time during the year when one can cut back as hard as one needs. Do not forget that this tree is an extremely vigorous grower.

Wiring can also be done at any time but is not always necessary.

General care

Watering
The bottle tree has very bulbous roots and trunk, and the ability to store supplies of water for drought conditions. It is one of the only trees that you can leave without water whilst you go on holiday.

All it will do if it gets dry is to cease growing. If it is dry during the winter it is also resistant to frost. When you water it, do so by immersing it in water and letting the moisture soak up.

Feeding
Nitrogenous food should be kept to a minimum and this tree should be fed with something like a tomato fertilizer during the growing season. If kept warm in the winter it will also need a smaller amount of the same.

Repotting
It can be repotted approximately every two to three years virtually at any time. You can encourage re-rooting with bottom heat.

Position
The bottle tree can be kept indoors throughout the year in virtually any position at all, although it is best to avoid cold draughts. Ideally it likes a nice bright window with plenty of light. Warmth is of little importance, but I would suggest an ideal temperature of between 5° C (41° F) and 24° C (75° F) Although considered something of a curiosity, the bottle tree makes an interesting addition to your bonsai collecion.

Common pests and diseases
None.

Sterculia approximately 6 years old, 30 cm (12 in) tall.

Styrax japonica

JAPANESE SNOWBALL

Informal Upright

Slanting

Semi-cascade

Broom

Raft

Group

Origins/type and description

This tree originates in China, Japan and Korea. It is regarded as a tender temperate tree, when grown as a bonsai.

Styrax is deciduous. Its leaves are a pointed oval and a rich green. Trunk and branches are smooth dark brown. It has the most beautiful white/pink bell-shaped flowers in early summer, which it bears in profusion, and they may be followed by small white fruits that give it the name of snowbell.

Propagation can be by seed or by cuttings taken in the late summer.

Training

General branch pruning can be carried out at any time. Finer pruning should only be done after the tree has finished flowering. Wiring is done during the growing season after flowering is over.

General care

Watering
Styrax needs moderate quantities of water during the summer but should be kept on the dry side during the winter. It has fleshy roots which if they are kept too wet can easily rot, and thus killing the tree.

Feeding
Feed every two weeks during the growing season, but not at all when it is dormant.

Repotting
Repotting is carried out in the early spring, every two or three years before growth appears. Remember to incorporate plenty of sharp sand and grit to improve the drainage.

Position
Although normally hardy when growing in the ground, it is advisable to protect styrax during periods of heavy frost. Keep in a bright position indoors but at an extremely cool temperature. Ideal winter temperature for styrax is 4–8° C (39–46° F). From early spring onwards, styrax should be placed outdoors, and only brought inside occasionally during the summer, for visitors to admire the flowers.

Common pests
Aphid; scale.

Styrax japonica approximately 15 years old, 46 cm (18 in) tall.

Tamarindus indica

TAMARIND

Informal Upright

Slanting

Group

Origins/type and description

This tree originates in Southern Asia, i.e. India, Philippines etc. It is tropical.

Tamarind is evergreen and has small pinnate leaves that remind one very much of mimosa. They are delicate, and tend to react against draughts etc, by dropping. The trunk is brown and interestingly smooth/rough. It is an ideal subject for bonsai, if care is taken. Roots normally spread out very evenly across the soil surface, giving the tree a very aged look.

Propagation is normally by seed.

Training

Pruning can be carried out at any time of the year, but always to a bud or a secondary branch. Leaf pruning is unnecessary.

Wiring can be done at any time during the growing season, but be careful not be bend the branches too strongly.

General care

Watering
During the growing period this tree needs ample water and it should be inspected evey day. It will also benefit from being sprayed with tepid water over the leaves.

Feeding
Feeding should be done at two weekly intervals throughout the growing season, and if in a very warm spot in the house during the winter, at three to four weekly intervals, but with a weaker solution.

Repotting
Repotting is necessary every two to three years with this variety. Good drainage material should be incorporated into the compost.

Position
Tamarind can be kept indoors the whole year round in a bright position that gets sunshine for one or two hours a day. Winter temperatures should be between 13° C (55° F) and 21° C (70° F). In the summer the tree can be placed outside for a rest but should be shaded from afternoon sunlight, and protected from strong winds.

Common pests
Scale; red spider mite.

Tamarindus indica *approximately 40 years old, 90 cm (36 in) tall.*

Zelkova sinica

(syn. *Ulmus parvifolia*)   CHINESE ZELKOVA

Informal Upright

Slanting

Semi-cascade

Broom

Clump

Raft

Group

Origins/type and description

This tree originates from China and is regarded as tender temperate to sub-tropical.

When cultivated in the warm, this tree will remain evergreen, but it will drop its leaves if the conditions are colder. It has small light to medium green leaves that are toothed at the edges. Normally the trunks are smooth and a grey brown in colour. Zelkova is a very strong grower and resistant to changes in growing conditions.

Propagation is by cuttings that are normally taken with a heel and treated with rooting hormone.

Training

Pruning can be carried out throughout the year, but in order that new branches can attain a certain amount of thickness, it is advisable to let the shoots grow at least eight to ten pairs of leaves before pruning back to one or two

Wiring can be done at any time during the growing season, but after the initial shape has been achieved it should be maintained by pruning.

General care

Watering
Keep moist at all times except during the winter when, if it is cool, watering can be cut down.

Feeding
Feed every two weeks during the summer, and every four weeks during the winter.

Repotting
This should be carried out every two to three years before the new spring growth commences. A good quality bonsai compost should be used and feeding should recommence approximately four weeks after repotting.

Position
This tree can be kept indoors throughout the year in a reasonably bright position. It is fairly tolerant about its temperature. A minimum should be regarded as 7° C (45° F) up to 22° C (70° F). As it is a strong tree, it will in fact, withstand slight frost, but if this happens then the tree will shed its leaves. During the summer it can be placed outside in almost any position.

Common pests and diseases
Aphid; red spider mite; black spot.

Zelkova sinica approximately 18 years old, 30 cm (12 in) tall.

124

Postscript

I hope this book has fired your imagination so that you will now try your hand at growing indoor bonsai trees. As you can see, the general cultural instructions are much the same for indoor bonsai as they are for ordinary houseplants: in both cases, it is essential that you remember to water and give the correct amount of fertilizer. Light source (natural or artificial) is also important. The actual training of a tree is not essential to the well being of the trees, except in regard to pruning, and the occasional repotting.

Although I have listed some of the more common styles for bonsai training, you are at perfect liberty to train the tree the way you want it to look. The most essential element of indoor bonsai is that it provides you and your family with pleasure. If you enjoy your trees you will look after them. In return they will give you many hours of interest and enjoyment.

Acknowledgements

All the colour photographs were taken by Bob Challinor.
All the line drawings, based on sketches by the author, were drawn by Peter Bull Art.

Index

Acacia dealbata, 58
Acer, 38
Acer trifidum, 53
Aerial roots, 10
Air layering, 32, 33
Aleppo pine, 10, 98
Ants, 55
Aphids, 54
Artificial lighting, 13, 21
Avocado, 30
Azalea, 21

Babylon, Hanging Gardens of, 8
Ballerina tree, 78
Banyan, 53, 76
Beech, 38
Beneficial fungus, 55
Bonsai, and topiary, 11
    appeal of, 11
    art form, 10
    cost, 10
    definition, 8
    grotesque shapes, 9, 10
    origins, 8–9
    twisted trunks, 10
    unnatural, 9
Botrytis, 55
Bottle tree, 38, 118
Bougainvillea, 21, 60–61
Box, 6, 62
Brassaia actinophylla, 114
Buddhist pine, 102
Buxus harlandii, 6, 22, 62

Californian juniper, 86
Cambium layer, 33, 35
Camellia sasanqua, 22, 64
Carmona microphylla, 13, 72
Caterpillar, 54
Central heating, 13, 14, 16, 21
Chian turpentine tree, 100
Chinese crape myrtle, 88
Chinese rock planting, 53
Chinese yew, 102
Chinese zelkova, 6, 13, 124
Chlorosis, 55
Citrus, 21, 30, 66
Clamps, 43
Coffea arabica, 30
Coffee, 30
Combined sprays, 56
Compost, consistency, 47
    functions, 46, 47
    ingredients, 48
    mix own, 47
Containers, colour, 51

decoration, 51
drainage, 50
glazing, 51
Crape myrtle, 88
Crassula aborescens, 21, 68
Crevice planting, 52
Cuttings, 30, 31
Cycas revoluta, 13, 70

Damping off, 55
Date palm, 30
Day length, 9, 13, 21
Display stand, 14
Downy mildew, 55
Draughts, 14, 22
Dry atmosphere, 14

Earwigs, 55
Egypt, pot plants in, 8
Ehretia buxifolia, 72
Emperor bonsai, 24
Eugenia brasiliensis, 21, 74

Fagus, 38
Feeding, 18, 19
    roots, 46
Fertilizers, 18, 19
    excess, 19–20
    insufficient, 19
    liquid, 19
    organic, 19
Ficus benjamina, 76
    brevifolia, 76
    carica, 22, 76
    diversifolia, 76
    falcata, 76
    infectoria, 76
    pumila var. minima, 76
    radicans, 76
Fig species, 8, 10, 13, 38, 53, 76
Firethorn, 108
Forest groups, 52
Fuchsia, 22, 78
Fukien tea, 72
Fungal diseases, 55
Fungicides, 56

Gardenia jasminoides, 80
Grafting, bud, 34
    root, 35
    side, 35
    top, 35
Grapefruit, 30, 66
Grey mould, 18
Gro Lights, 13

Hemp palm, 110
Hibiscus rosa-sinensis, 82
Holiday care, 20–21
Honeydew, 54
Humidifier, 14
Humidity, 18, 21

India, pot plants in, 8
Indoor bonsai, definition, 9
Indoor plants, 8
Insecticides, 56

Jacaranda mimosifolia, 13, 84
Jade plant, 68
Japanese snowball, 120
Jasmine orange, 90
Java willow, 10, 76
Juniper, 38, 40
    Californian, 38, 86
Juniperus californica, 21, 86

Kurrajong, 118
Kusamaki, 102

Lady's ear drops, 78
Lagerstroemia indica, 21, 88
Layering, 32, 33
Leaf miners, 55
Lemon, 30, 66
Light levels, 13, 21
Lime, 66
Litchi chinensis, 30
Little lady palm, 110
Lychee, 30

Mame, 24
Maple, 38
Mealy bug, 54
Mimosa, 58
Ming aralia, 104
Miniaturized plants, 9
Money tree, 68
Moss, 56
Murraya paniculata, 13, 90
Mycelium, 55
Myrtle, Common, 92
Myrtus communis, 92

Nandina domestica, 6, 21, 94
Nitrogen, 18

Olea europaea, 10, 21, 96
Olive, 10, 96
Orange, 30, 66
Outdoor rest, 13, 22

...mp, 110
...e lady, 110
Paper flower, 60–61
Persea americana, 30
Pests, 54, 55, 56
Phloem, 34
Phoenix dactylifera, 30
Phosphates, 18
Pines, 40
Pinus halepensis, 10, 21, 40, 98
Pistachio, 10, 21, 30, 100
Pistacia terebinthus, 10, 21, 30, 100
Plastic, covering with, 20
Podocarpus macrophyllus, 6, 21, 102
Polyscias fruticosa, 104
Pomegranate, 30, 106
Position in home, 14, 21–22
Potash, 18
Pot plants, 8
Powdery mildew, 55
Propagation, 30
Pruning, 9, 36, 38
    bud, 40
    leaf, 38
    root, 46
    where to cut, 40
Punicia granatum, 21, 30, 106
Pyracantha, 6, 22, 108

Queensland bottle tree, 118

Red spider mite, 54
Repotting, 46
    balanced look, 50
    containers, 50–51
    composts, 46, 47, 48, 49
    need for, 46
    position in pot, 50
    preparation, 46, 47
    removing from pot, 49
    technique, 49–50

timing, 46
    tying in, 50
    watering in, 50
    wiring in, 50
Rhapis humilis excelsa, 13, 110
Rock landscapes, 53
Rock plantings, 52–53
Root mealy bug, 54
Root pruning, 46
Rose of China, 82

Sacred bamboo, 94
Sageretia theezans, 13, 112
Sago palm, 70
Saikei, 9, 53
Scale insects, 55
Schefflera actinophylla, 13, 114
Scion, 34, 35
Sealing compounds, 38
Seasonal changes, 9
Seeds, 30
    for children, 30
Serissa foetida, 21, 116
Shade, provision of, 13, 14, 21, 50
Silver wattle, 58
Sizes, 24
Slugs and snails, 55
Sooty mould, 54
Sterculia rupestris, 13, 38, 118
Stock, 34, 35
Styles, 24
    Broom, 24
    Cascade, 24, 43
    Clump, 24, 27
    Formal upright, 24
    Group, 27
    Informal upright, 24
    Landscapes, 29
    Literati, 24
    Raft, 27
    Slanting, 24

Styrax japonica, 6, 22, 120
Sub-tropical trees, 21

Tamarind, 8, 13, 122
Tamarindus indica, 8, 13, 122
Tar oil wash, 56
Temperatures, 13, 21
Thimble, 24
Thrips, 55
Training, 42, 43
Tray landscapes, 53
Treating pests and diseases, 56
Tree of a thousand stars, 116
Trees, disposition of, 12–13
Trident maple, 53
Tropical trees, 13
Tying (to shape), 42

Ulmus parvifolia, 38, 124
Umbrella tree, 114

Virus, 55

Watering, 16, 18, 20, 21, 22
    drip, 20
    excessive, 18, 22
    immersion, 18
    insufficient, 18, 22
    wick, 20
Webs (red spider), 54
Weeping fig, 10
Weights (training), 42
White fly, 55
Wire, types of, 42
Wiring, 41, 42, 43
    branches, 43
    technique, 43
    time of day, 43
    trunk, 43
Woolly aphid, 54

Zelkova sinica, 6, 13, 38, 124